Special Edition 2007

By Mary Packard
and the Editors of Ripley Entertainment Inc.

Scholastic Inc.
New York   Toronto   London   Auckland   Sydney
Mexico City   New Delhi   Hong Kong   Buenos Aires

Library of Congress Cataloging-in-Publication data is available

ISBN 0-439-82598-9

Developed by Nancy Hall, Inc.
Edited by Linda Falken
Designed by Atif Toor and Iram Khandwala
Cover design by Kim Brown
Photo research by Carousel Research, Inc.
Index by Charles Carmony

12 11 10 9 8 7 6 5 4 3 2 1   6 7 8 9 10 11/0

Printed in China

First printing, September 2006

CONTENTS

SHOCK STAR

Do you like surprises? Are you attracted to the strange and unusual? Then step right up. You're about to enter the extraordinary world of Robert Ripley, a man who was as famous during his lifetime as any rock star of today. A self-taught cartoonist with a daily newspaper column, Ripley had a worldwide readership of over 80 million people. Each day, his mailbox was stuffed with 3,500 letters — and sometimes, he got more than letters. He once received a shrunken head with a note attached that said, "Please take good care of this. I think it is one of my relatives." Robert Ripley died in 1949, but his legacy lives on in the Ripley researchers who are always looking for new oddities to amaze and astound you.

Believe It!®

Crazy Critters

Augie, a golden retriever owned by the Miller family of Dallas, Texas, holds the doggy world record for picking up five tennis balls and holding them in his mouth — all at the same time!

The Inner You

Your own body is an amazing machine. Think about your heart, which pumps 700,000 gallons of blood a year! Or your liver, which can regenerate itself within a week — even if two-thirds of it have been surgically removed!

Odd-inary People

Zack Phillips is so dedicated to RollerSoccer he had hexagons tattooed on his head and dyes the hair inside to match the colors of whatever team he's rooting for!

CURI-ODD-ITIES

Ocean City, Maryland

Good to Go

During Robert Ripley's career, he traveled the USA and visited more than 200 other countries in search of all things weird and amazing — and did he ever find them! In 1933, he opened his first Odditorium at the Chicago World's Fair to display his collection. Today, there are more than 25 Odditoriums worldwide attracting millions of people. Many of the buildings are as odd as their exhibits!

RIPLEY FILE: 9.12.2003

Throughout this book, you'll see cartoons taken from the Ripley archives. The date that each cartoon was first published is shown at the top.

Creepy Stuff

The Dani people of Irian Jaya, Indonesia, used to smoke the bodies of certain village leaders. They kept the mummies, which are thought to have power and give protection to the villagers.

The World's Biggest . . .

Standing 40 feet tall and 13 feet wide, the world's largest broom was created in Deshler, Nebraska, to celebrate a broom factory's 50th anniversary. Later, it was dismantled and made into 1,440 regular-size brooms.

Special Attractions

In this edition of *Ripley's Special Edition 2007*, you'll find fun features, such as eye-popping optical illusions, "postcards" of unusual festivals, timelines about Deadheads (of State, that is), and milestone land speed records, from the first to the last.

. . . and the World's Smallest!

This miniature wooden replica of the Palace of Seventy-two Gables in the Forbidden City in Beijing, China, will fit nicely on a tabletop. Like the original, the replica was made without using nails.

We want your Believe It or Not! stories

If it's weird enough and if you would like to share it, the people at Ripley's would love to hear about it. You can send your *Believe It or Not!* entries to:

The Director of the Archives
Ripley Entertainment Inc.
7576 Kingspointe Parkway, Suite 188
Orlando, Florida 32819

1

WEIRD WORLD

Tall Web Site

In December 2004, it took Frenchman Alain Robert just four hours to scale Taiwan's Taipei 101 — the world's tallest building — despite high winds and rain. Due to the weather, Robert, who calls himself Spiderman, used ropes and a safety harness to climb the 1,667-foot-tall skyscraper. Normally, he prides himself on using only his hands and feet.

RIPLEY FILE: 11.29.2004

Duck and Cover! During a lunchtime debate over an 18-billion-dollar arms budget, Taiwanese legislators stopped eating and started a food fight, hurling everything from rice and veggies to hard-boiled eggs!

Strange Bedfellow

On April 16, 2003, an elderly couple in Espelkamp, Germany, got a rude awakening. A wild boar crashed through their patio doors, leaped into their bed, and burrowed under the covers, tusks and all! The boar was being chased by the couple's pet Yorkshire terrier. Andreas Janik, amazed that such a small dog could frighten a wild animal as large as a boar, had to smack the boar on the nose with a newspaper to get it to leave.

Slimed!

On October 12, 2003, millions of newly hatched millipedes swarmed over more than 1,300 feet of railroad track near Osaka, Japan, causing an oncoming train to skid to a stop, leaving a trail of squished bugs behind.

Riveting Ceremony

In Khochakandar, India, on the first weekend in June 2005, 400 wedding guests cheered while a band played Hindu songs and priests chanted Hindu prayers. Who were the bride and groom? Two giant toads! The wedding, arranged by local villagers, was an offering to the rain gods to get them to end a long dry spell.

October 13

The sky is filled with dinosaurs, motorcycles, sailboats, and more — a floating parade of hot-air balloons in the Special Shape Mass Ascension at the annual Albuquerque International Balloon Fiesta. At the Pole Grab Competition this morning, balloonists dipped, twisted, and turned to see who could retrieve the car keys from a 30-foot-tall pole — and win the new car! After sunset, hundreds of balloons, illuminated by their own fires, will light up the sky in a kaleidoscope of color.

Greetings from New Mexico!

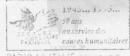

November 18

Here at Surin's Elephant Roundup festival, we actually watched a game of elephant soccer! Later on, we saw baby elephants parade with their mothers before judges. The prize for the most beautiful baby was a bunch of bananas. Later in the day, we cheered as an elephant had a tug-of-war against a hundred men. The elephant won and was rewarded with – what else? – more bananas!

Sa wah dee from Thailand!

February 28

We're standing in a sea of orange juice! Each year at Ivrea's Orange Festival, thousands of citizens celebrate the day that the town won its freedom from a tyrant in 1194. Volunteers drive chariots through the streets as mobs of "peasants" pelt the "cruel rulers" with thousands of oranges! Later, a young woman representing the heroine of the revolution rides through the streets throwing candy to spectators.

Ciao from Italy!

December 5

It's just after sunset in Küssnacht, and everyone is making a terrible racket! Why? It's Klausjagen Day — or time to chase Santa through the streets! The fun starts with a parade led by whip-crackers, followed by people carrying huge cut-out lanterns shaped like bishops' hats, Santa and his elves, and a brass band. Next come hundreds of people ringing cowbells or blowing horns, chased by the noisy mob. It all started in 1732 when villagers used noisemakers to chase away evil spirits. How Santa got mixed up in it, no one knows, but all agree it's a fun-filled way to start the holidays.

Guten Abend from Switzerland!

Major Tune-Up

In 1999, an "orchestra" of 100 bikers revved up their Harley-Davidson motorcycles at different volumes to play composer Staffan Mossenmark's latest offering. The outdoor concert took place in Stockholm, Sweden, where the bikers were led by conductor Petter Sundkvist, who waved racetrack flags instead of a baton. The title of the motorcycle masterpiece is *Wroom* — or, in English, *Vroom!*

RIPLEY FILE: 11.27.2004

Long-winded! DJ Barry Yip of Hong Kong, China, once spent 81 hours and 23 seconds singing 1,000 karaoke songs!

Wheel-y Naked

In 2004, activists around the world got together and organized protests against oil dependency and environmental pollution caused by automobile emissions. Instead of marching or holding sit-ins, however, the activists chose to ride bicycles — and instead of clothing, some wore body paint! Since then, the World Naked Bike Ride has become an annual event, with participants hitting the pedals as bare as they dare.

Pole on a Pole

In May 2002, Daniel Baraniuk of Gdańsk, Poland, climbed an 8-foot-tall pole onto a 16- by 24-inch platform and stayed there for 196 days and nights to set a new world record for pole-sitting.

"Phoney" Idea

In 2003, 10,000 people showed up at a park in London, England, to take part in the first Mobile Phone Olympics. The event featured such cell phone–related events as picture and text messaging, game playing, and cell-phone hurling contests. Eleven-year-old Reece Price won in all four categories — sending an 80-character text message in 56 seconds, sending a picture message in 21 seconds, scoring highest on the Tony Hawk's Pro Skater 4 cell-phone game, and hurling an old cell phone more than 113 feet.

Pinup Boys

In 2001, Kevin Thackwell (right) of Stoke-on-Trent, England, clipped 120 clothespins to his face, setting a new world record. That's a lot of clothespins, but quite not enough to hold onto the record for long. Garry "Stretch" Turner, whose rare deficiency of collagen makes his skin extremely stretchy, managed to clip 159 clothespins to his face — setting a new record in 2004!

Scotland

NORTH SEA

Denmark

Ireland

United Kingdom

England

Netherlands

Belgium

Germany

France

Switzerland

Aus

Italy

Portugal

Spain

ATLANTIC OCEAN

4

2

1

1 Spain: Even though construction began on La Sagrada Familia in Barcelona, Spain, 125 years ago, it will be another 30 to 80 years before the church is completed. Still, more than two million people a year flock to see its tall towers (there will eventually be 18, the tallest of them 558 feet high) and admire its fanciful stonework. The architect, Antoni Gaudi, worked on the church for most of his life, from age 31 until his death in 1926 at age 74 — and his body is entombed there.

2 Italy: If you visit La Specola before lunch, you may not feel like eating afterward! This museum in Florence is famed for its huge collection of anatomically correct wax figures in various stages of such nasty illnesses as the bubonic plague!

3 Austria: Hellbrunn Castle, built in the 1600s, is famous for its trick fountains that soak unsuspecting visitors. Just as ingenious are its water-driven mechanical figures. In the castle's theater, 200 of them act out scenes from everyday life in an 18th-century town. Others, including the Germaul (right), which is the secret emblem of Hellbrunn, are hidden in grottos around the grounds.

4 England: Each summer, thousands of visitors flock to York for a chance to get lost in one of the world's largest mazes! They wander among 30 acres of paths cut through 1.5 million ten-foot-tall maize (corn) plants that would confuse even someone with the best sense of direction.

5 Slovakia: Unlike most one-street towns, Medzilaborce boasts a museum of modern art. You can't miss it — two giant sculptures, *Campbell's Soup I* and *Campbell's Soup II*, sit just outside the doors. The museum is dedicated to the art of Andy Warhol, whose mother, Julia, was born nearby.

Poland

ech public

Slovakia

5

4

Hungary

Croatia

Romania

Bosnia and Herzegovina

Yugoslavia

Macedonia

Albania

Greece

BALTIC SEA

MEDITERRANEAN SEA

STRANGE STRUCTURES

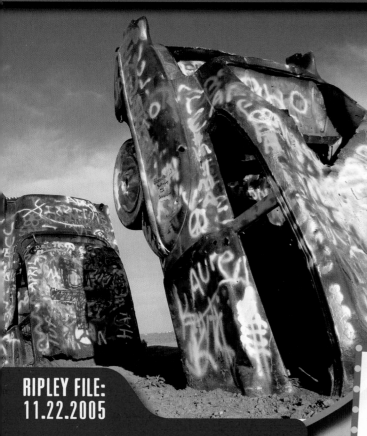

RIPLEY FILE:
11.22.2005

Desert Gem! A monument in Quartzite, Arizona, honors Hadji Ali, the Syrian camel handler who oversaw the United States Camel Corps in the American West during the 1850s.

Bird Calls

If you're ever in the city of Guaira, Brazil, you can phone home from a public phone shaped like a toucan. The region's most endangered species, the toucan will soon be extinct if steps are not taken to protect it. The toucan phone booth is a sharp reminder of what would be lost should this magnificent bird ever vanish from the Earth.

Shimmering City

Sculptor Liz Hickok of San Francisco, California, created a scale model of her home city out of molded Jell-O! Before the dramatically lit, brightly colored buildings and bridges dissolved into puddles of colored water, Hickok recorded them for posterity in photographs and videos. In the latter, she makes the buildings shake, just like an earthquake — or a bowlful of jelly!

Double-time

A church in Xaghra, Malta, has twin clock towers — one shows the correct time, while the other is kept still to fool the devil.

Can-struction

This incredible replica of the Basilica of Saint Peter in Rome, Italy, was constructed entirely from used soft-drink cans — 10 million of them to be exact! Measuring 316 feet wide and 97 feet high, the replica was built in 1997 by volunteers. It remained intact for just one year, after which it was dismantled and the metal auctioned off for charity.

Cutting-Edge Exhibits

The British Lawnmower Museum in Southport, England, features more than 200 exhibits of antique and unique mowing implements, including a lawn mower that once belonged to Prince Charles and Princess Diana.

Token of Depreciation

In 1975, a coin, thought to have been a relic dating back to the Roman Empire, was displayed in the British Museum in London, England. A few days later, a nine-year-old girl pointed out that the prominent R engraved on the coin did not stand for Roma, but rather for Robinson's — a soft-drink company that gave away the tokens as an advertising gimmick.

HEIGHT OF FASHION

It's a bird! It's a plane! No, it's a fashion model! On July 27, 2005, the Target retail chain turned the fashion world upside down with its vertical fashion show. Wearing Target's autumn clothing line and steel harnesses, a troupe of trained athletes leaped from the roof of a tower in New York City's Rockefeller Plaza, then strutted down the side of the building to the shocked delight of spectators.

Deep Thoughts

The Retretti Art Centre in Punkaharju, Finland, is unique in that nearly 40,000 square feet of its space is carved from a labyrinth of caves. Critics have called it the world's most amazing art gallery and music hall in the world. The Retretti's underground concert site, which holds 800 people, has been the setting for a wide variety of music, from jazz to rock to opera.

Pachyderm Paradise

In 2005, 65 elephants got a break from their job of hauling heavy logs in Tamil Nadu, India, when they were sent to elephant camp for 48 days of rest and relaxation. There they were able to enjoy the fresh air, eat special highly nutritious food, and bathe in the river — where they were scrubbed clean by Mahouts (elephant trainers).

Hairy Solution

The police in northern India didn't think they were getting the respect they deserved. So the chief of police of Madhya Pradesh province did some homework. His research turned up a study concluding that police officers who had mustaches were taken more seriously than those who didn't — so the police chief has offered pay raises to policemen who grow mustaches. Problem solved!

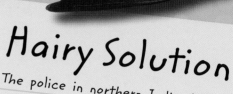

Purr-fect Choice

The United Nations has named world-famous cartoon character Hello Kitty as the official representative of UNICEF (United Nations Children's Fund). A special event was held to mark the anniversary of UNICEF in New York on June 8, 2004, and to welcome their new partner in raising awareness of the plight of children around the world.

High-tech Tag

Students at New York University's Interactive Telecommunications Program are earning graduate credits by bringing Pac-man, a 1980s video game, to life. They call it Pac-Manhattan. To play, you need five players and five controllers. Pac-man's job is to collect all the virtual dots that run the length of the streets in Greenwich Village's Washington Square Park before the four ghosts, Inky, Blinky, Pinky, and Clyde, can catch him or her. The whole chase is tracked on the Internet by the controllers, who guide the players by using cell phones and updating their positions on a software map. Pac-man knows how many dots have been "eaten" by talking to his or her controller.

2

NATURAL WONDERS

Smashing Success!

On July 4, 2005, the fireworks on Earth were nothing compared to the light show in space! That's when the spaceship *Deep Impact* hurled a missile at Tempel 1, a four-mile-wide comet. Traveling at 23,000 miles per hour, the 820-pound missile blasted a huge hole in the comet's surface to help scientists find out what Tempel 1 was made of. Most of the data is still being analyzed, but there has already been one major surprise: It seems the exterior of a comet is not hard, as previously thought, but soft and fine like talcum powder! Who knew?

Asteroid Slams Earth!

By October 2005, NASA scientists logging Near-Earth Objects (NEOs) had found more than 3,500. One of them, a 1,000-foot-wide asteroid called Apophis, may actually crash into Earth in 2036. Not to worry, however. Apophis probably wouldn't cause as much damage as the 4- to 7-mile-wide asteroid believed to have struck Earth 250 million years ago. That one nearly caused the extinction of all life on Earth.

Did you know everyone on Earth is moving at more than 67,000 miles per hour as our planet rotates on its axis and orbits the sun?

Way Out!

In July 2005, astronomers announced the discovery of Object 2003UB$_{313}$ — nicknamed Xena (after TV's warrior princess) — beyond Pluto. Like Pluto, it's covered with frozen methane and has a moon, but it's about 30 percent larger. Xena's discoverers think it should be classified as the tenth planet, but the jury's still out. Why? Scientists have never officially defined what a planet is! Luckily, this hasn't stopped anyone from studying Xena. Among the discoveries are that it orbits the sun once every 560 years.

Is Anybody Out There?

Unidentified flying objects (UFOs), alien abductions, secret government communications with extraterrestrials — all assume that there are other life-forms in the universe. Do extraterrestrials really exist? That's the question scientists at the SETI (Search for Extraterrestrial Intelligence) Institute in Berkeley, California, are trying to answer. They use radio telescopes to listen for unidentified signals that could be sent by extraterrestrials. Some of the signals are analyzed by SETI@home, a virtual supercomputer consisting of thousands of PCs connected to the Internet — it's a project that anyone who owns a computer can participate in.

DOWN TO EARTH

On Solid Ground?

Think again. Imagine Earth as an egg. The thickness of Earth's crust — the eggshell — varies from about 3 miles to 43 miles. The crust is broken up into large pieces called tectonic plates. These plates "float" above the mantle — the egg white — which is about 1,800 miles thick. Most of the mantle is hot, thick, molten rock. Below the mantle is Earth's core — the yolk. About 1,400 miles of the core is molten metals, while only the inner part, about 750 miles in diameter, is solid. As Earth rotates, the liquid mantle roils around. This movement, together with heat and pressure, forces the tectonic plates to move apart or crash together, causing earthquakes and volcanic eruptions — and building mountains!

Monster Mushroom

What lives up to 3 feet underground, covers 3.5 miles, and is at least 2,400 years old? It's a humongous fungus! Its scientific name is *Armillaria ostoyae*, but it's also called the honey mushroom. Scientists first discovered it when they were trying to figure out why trees were dying in a section of Oregon's Malheur Forest. (The French word *malheur* means "misfortune.") The fungus puts out tentacles that penetrate the wood, then fan out under the bark, taking water and nutrients — and, incidentally, killing the trees.

Rock Legends

Here are some hard facts and some very old myths that are hardly rock solid!

Turquoise
Fact: Turquoise gets its color from the mineral copper.
Legend: Native Americans wore turquoise during dry spells because they believed that it could bring rain.

Aquamarine

Fact: Aquamarine crystals can weigh up to 243 pounds.
Legend: People with enemies kept these stones around in case they were poisoned. For an instant "cure," they'd grind up the crystals and stir them into a cup of tea.

United States

Pakistan

Amethyst

Fact: Lovely amethyst crystals are found inside rough, chunky rocks called geodes.
Legend: People who needed to keep a clear head wore amethysts to stay awake and alert.

Brazil

Tanzania

Australia

Garnet

Fact: Garnets come in more colors than any other mineral — every color but blue.
Legend: For sweet dreams, people suffering from nightmares tucked garnets under their pillows.

Opal

Fact: Opals get their iridescent quality from a mineral called silica.
Legend: People once believed wearing opals made them invisible.

LOW LIVES

Lightheaded

The female anglerfish doesn't have to hunt for her meals. She simply relies on the bulblike lure filled with light-producing bacteria on the top of her head to attract fish for dinner.

RIPLEY FILE:
5.06.1972

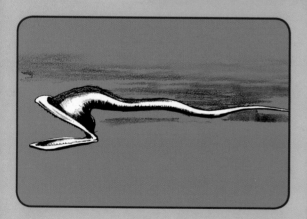

Gulp! The pelican eel can live at depths of 6,500 feet or more. Also known as the gulper eel, it can stretch its loosely hinged jaws and gullet to swallow fish much larger than itself.

Gutless Wonders

Giant tubeworms thrive near hydrothermal vents. They have no eyes, mouths, or intestines. One end of the tube is attached to the ocean floor, and at the other end is a red plume used for breathing. The worms eat hydrogen sulfide gas that has been converted into nutrients by the bacteria that live inside the worms' bodies.

Lights Out!

The deep-sea shrimp can emit a cloud of light from its mouth to temporarily blind or distract a predator, allowing the shrimp to disappear into darker water.

Great Balls of Snot

When scientists began exploring the ocean floor, they were surprised by how much life was there — and by how little food there was to sustain it. In 1972, a marine scientist named Alice Alldredge suggested the answer might be mucus "houses" — or, in other words, snot — called sinkers, and recent studies have confirmed it. Sinkers are produced by tadpole-like animals called giant larvaceans. About 2 inches long, a larvacean spins a mucus web roughly 3 feet in diameter, sits inside it, and uses it to filter small bits of food. When the filter gets plugged up by sea creatures and other food too big to fit through, the larvacean moves out, and the sinker falls to the ocean floor like a carton full of takeout. Dinner is served!

Smokin'!

Deep under the oceans, tall towers rise up like underwater skyscrapers. These towers are called hydrothermal vents, or black smokers. They're formed when scalding water, laden with sulfur and other minerals and gases, bubbles up from deep inside Earth and breaks through the ocean floor. When this superhot stuff hits cold water, the minerals harden and the towers grow taller and taller — some as high as 160 feet.

Tree-mendous!

A 1,500-year-old boab tree in Derby, Australia, was used during the 1890s as an overnight jail! The hollow Prison Tree, with a diameter of 46 feet, has a hole cut in its side for an entrance. Boab trees have been known to store hundreds of gallons of water in their trunks.

Long Distance

A solar system is a group of planets that circle a star. A galaxy is larger and includes a multitude of stars and gases all held together by gravity. The Milky Way contains about 100 billion stars. Our sun is one of them. It would take the SR-71 Blackbird, the world's fastest jet, 5.1 *billion years* to get from one end of the Milky Way to the other. That must be why they call it space!

Rooted Out

This strange-looking pine tree stands six feet tall. That's not so big, unless you consider that it's actually not a tree but the root structure of what used to be a tree. The ground around the real tree was eroded by wind and rain, exposing the huge root system that was once entirely underground.

TIME AND SPACE

On August 16, 2005, the Russian Cosmonaut Sergei Krikalev logged 748 days in orbit, setting a new record for the most cumulative time in space. At the time, Krikalev was the commander of the International Space Station. In the past, he spent time on the Mir Space Station and was a crew member on the space shuttle *Discovery*.

Lasting Impression

The first people ever to set foot on the moon were *Apollo 11* astronauts Neil Armstrong and Edwin "Buzz" Aldrin. That was back in 1969, but their footprints are still there. That's because wind and rain don't exist on the moon, so there's nothing to disturb them. In fact, it's possible the astronauts' footprints will stay there forever!

Gold Flush!

When Antarctica's Mount Erebus erupts, what comes out is not ordinary molten lava. Within the flow are particles of pure gold!

Rock On!

Ejected centuries ago from a now-extinct volcano near Soriano nel Cimino, Italy, the giant boulder known as Sasso Menicante is 30 feet long and weighs 276 tons — yet it is so well balanced on its narrow base that it can rock back and forth without ever falling off.

In Depth

Most people think that outer space is the only new frontier. However, even though oceans cover 71 percent of Earth, we know more about the surface of the moon than we do about the planet's ocean floor. Not only is Earth's deepest ravine (Mariana Trench, 35,640 feet deep) underwater, but also its longest mountain range (the Mid-Ocean Ridge, 31,000 miles long). Even with today's technology, it would still take scientists about 125 years just to make a map of it!

Ring Cycle

Many people already know that if you cut down a tree, the number of rings in the trunk can tell you how old the tree is — each ring counts for one year. However, did you know that the rings on the south-facing side of the trunk are slightly farther apart than the ones on the northern side? So if you were to get lost in a dark forest without a compass, it would be helpful to have a chain saw and a flashlight!

3

CLASS ACTS

TOO COOL!

Ramping Up

On July 9, 2005, skateboarding superstar Danny Way rolled down a huge ramp at nearly 50 miles per hour and jumped across the Great Wall of China, becoming the first person to clear the wall without motorized aid!

RIPLEY FILE:
10.17.2004

Swept Away! In 2003, 43-year-old Raphaëla le Gouvello of France became the first woman to windsurf almost 5,000 miles across the Pacific Ocean. Undaunted by the triple threats of seasickness, the cold, and hungry sharks, she completed the trip in 89 days. The ocean from Lima, Peru, to Tahiti is the most isolated stretch of water in the world.

High Time!

In 1891, a baker named Sylvain Dornon from a marshy area of France called Les Landes, strapped on his stilts in Paris and started walking. Fifty-eight days and 2,000 miles later, he arrived in Moscow, setting a record for stilt-walking that's still unbroken!

Winging It

On July 31, 2003, extreme thrill seeker Felix Baumgartner of Austria pulled off the impossible. Wearing nothing but a jumpsuit, an oxygen tank, a 6-foot carbon-fiber wing strapped to his back, and a parachute for landing, he jumped out of a plane at 30,000 feet and glided 22 miles across the English Channel! Then he pulled the rip cord on his parachute and floated to terra firma in Calais, France. The whole trip took just 14 breathtaking minutes.

On a Roll

In September 2003, near Berlin, Germany, champion in-line skater Jürgen Köhler hitched a ride on a motorcycle — a very fast one! Hanging on to the back of a Suzuki Hayabusa as the driver floored it, Köhler reached a speed of 175 miles per hour on his custom-built skates!

YOU'RE KIDDING!

RIPLEY FILE:
4.13.2004

Underage Driver!
David Higgins of Suffolk, England, hit a 105-yard hole in one — and he was only four years old!

Ticket Masters

What would you do if you found 66 tickets to a major-league playoff game lying on the ground? It happened to a group of seventh graders on their way home from school in Summit, New Jersey. The box-seat tickets were worth $20,000! Sure, it would have been fun to take all their friends to the game. Instead, the boys turned the tickets in to the police, who returned them to their rightful owner — the Wachovia Bank. The boys and their parents were rewarded with luxury seats to a New Jersey Nets game, and Yankees owner George Steinbrenner sent them tickets to a Yankees game as well. When it comes to honesty, these kids are batting a thousand!

Queen of the Sea

In 1926, 19-year-old Gertrude Ederle of New York became the first woman to swim across the English Channel. She did it in 14 hours and 31 minutes, breaking the men's record by over two hours and setting a new one that stood for 24 years!

Diamond Girl

Every pitcher dreams of pitching a perfect game. On July 7, 2005, the National Baseball Hall of Fame paid tribute to an 11-year-old who did just that. Katie Brownell, the only girl in her upstate New York Little League, had been pitching for her team, the Dodgers, for three years. On May 14, 2005, she struck out all 18 batters she faced, leading her team to an 11 – 0 victory. At the special ceremony to honor her, Katie donated her perfect-game jersey to the Baseball Hall of Fame in Cooperstown, New York. You might say that Katie Brownell is pitcher perfect.

Gum Ho!

Blowing bubbles can be profitable as well as fun! Every year, kids under twelve compete in local contests all over the USA to see who can blow the biggest bubble. Eventually, the field is narrowed to five finalists, who travel to New York City for the Dubble Bubble National Blowing Contest where the winner takes home $10,000 worth of savings bonds! Aina-Soe Cambridge (right) of Chicago, Illinois, won in 2003 with a 14-inch bubble.

Gut Course

The room is stocked with gun powder, vials of fake blood, carpet fiber samples, and dental records. No, they're not props from a detective show. They're school supplies. Within months of Court TV's 2002 launch of its Forensics in the Classroom project, more than 22,000 high school teachers had signed up for the free lesson plans. Developed with the help of the American Academy of Forensic Sciences, the lessons start with a crime scene. To solve the mystery, students collect evidence, take measurements and fingerprints, analyze "blood" spatters, stains, and fibers — and along the way, learn a lot about biology, math, technology, and other scientific concepts.

RIPLEY FILE:
3.17.2003

Sweet Deal! Students at the Falkenberg High School of Design in southwestern Sweden are paid the equivalent of $60 a month just to show up at school on time every day.

Payne-free Classes

Designed by former race car driver Jeff Payne, Driver's Edge is a free driving program for teens. It's based on the idea that no one is better equipped than a race car driver to teach the skills new drivers need to avoid becoming a statistic. Kids learn not to panic when a car goes into a skid by experiencing one firsthand — over and over again — until the appropriate response becomes second nature. Hair-raising maneuvers are learned in a traffic-free, controlled environment. Ironically, students taught by professional speedsters usually graduate with a healthy respect for speed!

Heights and Depths

As an incentive to get them to stop playing hooky, students at Bonny Doon School in Edmonton, Canada, were offered a ride in a hot-air balloon and a diving lesson.

Real Cold Case

Think students can't make a difference? Tell that to the parents of James Chaney, Michael Schwerner, and Andrew Goodman, three young civil rights workers who were murdered in June 1964. Forty years later, Sarah Siegel, Allison Nichols, and Brittany Saltiel, students at Adlai E. Stevenson High School in Lincolnshire, Illinois, made a documentary about the unsolved case for a history project. They interviewed the boys' families then traveled to Mississippi to talk to one of the suspected killers, Edgar Ray Killen. The students used the evidence they gathered to get the case reopened. The result? Killen was convicted and will spend the rest of his life in jail.

RIPLEY'S NEWS

Baring It All

HAMPSHIRE, ENGLAND: It took 44-year-old Stephen Gough 11 months to walk 900 miles from one end of Great Britain to the other. Neither rain, near-freezing temperatures, nor a few nights in jail could stop him. Why was he arrested? They don't call him the Naked Rambler for nothing — Gough made the whole trip without wearing any clothes!

Wheel-y Silly!

OVIEDO, SPAIN: Lawyer Álvaro Neil sold his car and bought a more economical form of transportation — a bicycle. In 2001, he set off to pedal more than 18,000 miles through South America. Then in 2004, Neil quit his job and began a bike ride around the world. Starting in Africa, he'll move on to the Middle East, Asia, and Australia, then fly to Alaska and pedal to Argentina's Tierra del Fuego before returning to Europe. Oh, yes, and during the entire trip, he'll be dressed as a clown!

Hot Act

ALLAHABAD, INDIA: Rajendra Kumar Tiwari entertains audiences by balancing up to a dozen candles in his mustache — lit candles, that is. Then he strikes up the band and, using the muscles in his face, makes his mustache and the lit candles dance to the strains of Indian music. In order to improve muscle control, he even had two teeth pulled. When he's not performing, Tiwari collects things other people throw away and finds a place for them in his waste museum.

Scorpion Queen

KUANTAN, MALAYSIA: On September 19, 2004, Nur Malena Hassan celebrated her 27th birthday in a shopping center. She wasn't shopping, however, but living in a 10-by-12-foot glass room — with 6,069 scorpions! Why? She wanted to reclaim the world record she'd set in 2001 for the longest stay with scorpions — 30 days with 2,700 of the poisonous creatures — which had been beaten by a Thai woman in 2002. After 36 days and 17 painful stings, Hassan was proud to once again be named the Scorpion Queen.

Sailing Around!

USHANT, FRANCE: Twenty-eight-year-old Ellen MacArthur of Great Britain completed her 27,354-mile circumnavigation of the globe in a 75-foot-long trimaran — alone! — on February 7, 2005. The voyage lasted 71 days, 14 hours, 18 minutes, and 33 seconds — setting a new world record for a solo voyage around the world.

Casting a Spell

Ornicopytheobibliopsychocrystarroscioae-
rogenethliometeoroaustrohieroanthropoich-
thyopyrosiderochpnomyoalectryoophiobo-
tanopegobydrorhabdocrithoaleuroalphitoh-
alomolybdoclerobeloaxinocoscinodactyliogeoli-
thopessopsephocatoptrotephraoneirochiroony-
chodactyloarithstichooxogeloscogastrogyroce-
robletonooenosapulinaniac. When nine-year-old
Aaron Zweig of Randolph, New Jersey, spelled
this word, his fourth-grade teacher nearly fell
off her chair. Aaron surprised her by spelling the
309-letter word — which was used in the Middle
Ages to describe someone who can predict the
future — without a single mistake!

On the Ball

Anyone who's ever tried juggling knows that it's harder than it looks. However, Dave Finnigan, creator of the Juggling for Success school program, guarantees that if you practice, you'll not only learn to juggle but also gain self-confidence and improve your academic performance in reading, writing, and math. Teachers in the more than 400 elementary schools that use this classroom-based program agree.

Big Rip-Off

In August 2004, it took 69-year-old Ed Charon of Oregon just three minutes to reclaim the record for phone-book ripping by tearing in half 39 directories, each one 1,004 pages thick!

Barking Up the Right Tree

According to a recent study conducted by German psychologist Reinhold Bergler, children who own dogs are better behaved, more motivated, and get better grades than children who don't. *Woof! Woof!*

Starbucks Joe

So far, John Winter Smith of Silver Spring, Maryland, is well on his way to fulfilling his dream — to visit every company-owned Starbucks store in the world. Since 1997, he's collected cups from almost 5,000 stores in North America and more than 200 in other countries, which he uses to create fanciful sculptures. Smith has gained a certain amount of fame for his unusual pastime, appearing on CBS's *The Early Show*, NPR radio, and CNN *Headline News*.

Real Eye-opener

"Bullet" Bob Oldham of Myrtle Beach, South Carolina, can open beer bottles with his eyebrows.

Puck Pluck

The Seeing Ice Dogs are a hockey team located in Calgary, Canada. Why the odd name? It just so happens that most of the players on the team are blind!

Dress-ing the Part

Rupert Grint wanted to be in the film version of *Harry Potter* so badly that he auditioned as a girl, hoping to stand out from the thousands of other kids who auditioned for the part of Ron Weasley. Rupert knew that Ron wasn't a girl, but he thought that dressing as one might get him noticed. It did — and he got the part!

Easy as Pi?

The ratio of the circumference of a circle to its diameter has an infinite number of decimal places. It's called pi, and most people stop at 3.14159 — but not everybody. In July 2005, 59-year-old Akira Haraguchi, a psychiatric counselor from Chiba, Japan, spent 11 hours reciting the first 83,431 decimal places from memory! Why did he do it? To break the previous record — his own — of 54,000 numerals.

4

ODD GALLERY

BODY ODD-IFICATION

Painted Lady

Great Britain's Isobel Varley is covered from head to toe in colorful tattoos. Varley got her first tattoo in 1986 at age 49, and from then on she was hooked. In fact, she began getting piercings as well. Now she travels the world to show off her body art, appearing on TV shows and speaking at tattoo conventions. Called the World's Most Tattooed Senior Woman, this proud title-holder has no plans to stop getting painted any time soon!

RIPLEY FILE:
1.25.2004

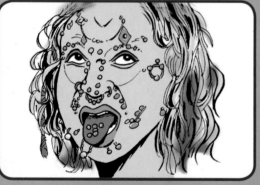

Poke-r Face! In 2003, Elaine Davidson of Edinburgh, Scotland, achieved the goal she had been shooting for all her adult life — to be the world's most pierced woman. At that time, she had 1,903 body piercings. As of August 2004, she claimed 2,520 piercings. Ouch!

Out of Shape

Garry "Stretch" Turner of Holton le Moor, England, has a rare condition called Ehlers-Danlos syndrome, which affects the connective tissues. What does that mean? His skin is stretchy — so stretchy that he can even pull the skin of his neck up over his mouth. In fact, Turner holds the world record for having the stretchiest skin.

Needle Man!

In 1993, Bernard Moeller of Pennsylvania set the world record for the most individual tattoos — a staggering 14,000!

Kick in the Head

In 1996, Zack Phillips of San Francisco created the RollerSoccer International Federation to promote the sport — playing soccer on in-line skates — he'd invented the year before. Phillips even turned his head into a soccer ball. To save time, he had the hexagons tattooed on his head so that all he has to do is dye the hair within the lines. He also dyes his eyebrows and beard to match. Sometimes Phillips will let another fan touch his head, but kicking is strictly forbidden!

Hairy-copter

In October 2004, hairstylists from all over the country gathered at the Apollo Theater in New York City to show off their work. Although there were no winners or losers at the exhibition, called Hair Wars, the stylists did their best to *outdo* one another. Hairstylist Mr. Little of Detroit, Michigan, scored a major hit with his creation of a helicopter made out of hair. Equipped with flashing lights and a rotating propeller, this hairdo was battery operated!

**RIPLEY FILE:
12.29.1996**

Monumental Mop! In the 1500s BCE, the ancient Assyrians cut their hair in the shape of tiered pyramids.

Top-coat

In ancient Rome, bald men frequently painted hair onto their scalps.

Traffic Stopper

It takes a lot to stop traffic in New York City, but model Keisha Caesar did just that, creating a traffic jam as she walked from the hair salon to the Hair Wars exhibition at the Apollo Theater. A cab driver actually stopped his car to gawk at her head. Created by Veronica Forbes, the hairdo was inspired by the headgear of a fellow churchgoer.

Heads Up

In February 2003, many of Russia's most breathtaking sights were recreated — not on canvas or in stone — but on the heads of runway models! At the annual Hairdressers, Nail Art, and Body Art Designers contest held in St. Petersburg, spectators got to see some unbelievable creations. From buildings in Moscow's Red Square to the most famous bridge in St. Petersburg, nothing was too elaborate to be made into a hairdo!

49

NASTY!

RIPLEY FILE:
3.03.2000

BURP!

Take Cover! A Colorado company named Excuse Me makes a super-fizzy soda called Rudy Begonia's Belcher that's guaranteed to deliver explosively loud belches.

How Charming!

On April 29, 2002, Dudu Miah, a snake charmer in Bangladesh was called to a house to get rid of some poisonous cobras living beneath the floorboards. He dug up more than 3,000 baby snakes and feasted on more than a dozen of them.

Slug-fest

In 1982, Ken Edwards of Cheshire, England, ate 12 live slugs, followed by 2 steel wool soap pads for dessert — in less than 2 minutes!

Crispy Critters

Scorpions, water beetles, bamboo worms, grasshoppers, and other such creatures have long been a staple food of Thailand's northern provinces. In 2002, Satapol Polprapas, an ex-shrimp farmer, and his partner, Pailin Thanomkait, launched Insect Inter, a fast-food company specializing in cooked bugs served with chili sauce and other condiments. Even better, the company is planning to can their tasty bug bites and ship them all over the world!

Good Grub

Long a native food source in Australia's outback, witchetty grubs, the larvae of the ghost moth, are highly nutritious and rich in both calcium and iron. Just ten a day of these tasty grubs, which live in the roots of the witchetty bush, are sufficient for survival. Definitely an acquired taste, the grubs are said to have an almondlike flavor. Some Australians eat them raw. Others like them barbecued or made into a soup.

CRAZY CONTESTS

RIPLEY FILE:
8.08.1932

Rock   Paper

Scissors

Hand-out! Established in 1918, the World RPS Society based in Toronto, Canada, holds an annual contest to pick the new Rock Paper Scissors World Champion!

Grime Game

In 1999, Tide held a Dirtiest Kid in America contest. The twelve finalists got to travel to New York City and compete in the Stain-a-Thon Showdown at Grand Central Station. The kids had to tackle an obstacle course where they climbed a "mountain" covered in chocolate sauce and whipped cream, plunged down a peanut butter and jelly slide, and were tossed into a mound of chocolate pudding. Nine-year-old Ben James of Chesterfield, Missouri, took home the prize: a trip to Disney World and $500.

Fingerhold

On July 25, 2004, the town of Rimbach, Germany, hosted the Alpine Finger Draw Hook championships. The object of the competition? To drag your opponent across a table by a leather ring held by only one finger. Ouch!

Odd-lympics

At Alaska's annual Eskimo-Indian Olympics, participants in the Ear Weight contest vie to see who can walk the longest distance with 16 one-pound lead ingots tied to one ear.

That Takes the Cake!

On June 7, 2005, New York City's Times Square was a blur of white. No, it wasn't an unseasonable snowstorm but something just as bizarre — a wild contest sponsored by the creators of a television show called *Bridezilla*. To win $50,000, 20 brides dressed in their wedding dresses had to dive into a giant cake to search for the cash. The consolation prize? A face full of cake!

BIG SHOTS

Big Foot

You'd have to be a giant to fit into Canada's 80,000-pound boot! Made out of fiberglass, the 39-foot-tall boot was definitely not made for walking! Rather, it was built in 1987 in Edmonton, Alberta, to attract customers to Canada's Western Boot Factory. With such a colossal landmark, the factory would be easy to find. Nevertheless, all that remains of the company today is this super-sized boot.

Big Hitter

You know you're approaching Kentucky's Louisville Slugger Museum when you spot the giant baseball bat that leans against it. The world's largest bat weighs in at 34 tons and reaches many feet above the five-story building. A replica of the Louisville Slugger, a 34-inch wooden bat used by Babe Ruth in the 1920s, the big bat is made of hollow carbon steel.

Wheel-y Big!

It takes three days, $30,000, and enough rubber for 5,276 car tires to make a single one of the world's largest tires, which are used on 250,000-pound front-end-loader Caterpillar trucks.

Burying the Big One

The world's largest tomahawk is located in Cut Knife, Saskatchewan, Canada. Fashioned from a fir log measuring 54 feet long, the handle alone weighs 12,000 pounds! The immense tomahawk was erected in 1971 as a symbol of the unity and friendship among the Native American First Nations and the other communities in the region.

Big Seater

Imagine the world's biggest family reunion. You would need a lot of seats. That's exactly what the builders of this super-sized sofa had in mind when they created it for the 1999 annual Dubai Shopping Festival — whose theme just happened to be "The Family Get-together of the Millennium." At 108 feet, the sofa's length easily surpasses that of the previous record holder, a 24-foot-long sofa built by a British furniture company. Three-and-half-year-old Vishal Venkat shows his approval by bouncing on the Dubai sofa's massive cushions.

EXTRA! EXTRA!

Cart-a-goons

Instead of being pulled by dogsleds as in the Iditarod Trail Sled Dog Race in Alaska, competitors in the Idiotarod Race wear the most idiotic costumes they can find while pushing outrageously decorated shopping carts. The 5-mile race through the streets of New York City features teams dressed as ghostbusters, Mexican mariachis, and giant squids, to name a few. Why do they do it? Answers one participant, "For the glory and the chance to win 300 dollars."

Red Alert

In 2002, to cut down on roadkill and help preserve Australia's declining koala population, officials in Brisbane painted koala carcasses red and left them on the side of the road for motorists to see. The idea was to shock drivers into slowing down. Conservation groups estimate that only 20 percent of the koala's natural habitat remains and place the koala population at fewer than 100,000.

Cutting-Edge Sport

At the annual Chain-saw Chuck competition in Whitehorse, Alaska, competitors hurl chain saws as far as they can throw them — some reaching a distance of 55 feet! Spectators, stand back!

RRRRRRRR

RAW DEAL

Young women from the Banda tribe in the Central African Republic are not considered ready for marriage until they have eaten an entire chicken — raw — without breaking any bones!

56

Unbelievable!

Gordon Zwicky's tale begins when he and his wife win the lottery and use the money to drive to Florida. Along the way, they spot a highway sign that reads CLEAN RESTROOMS AHEAD. Since Zwicky believes in obeying road signs, the couple ends up using 267 rolls of paper towels, 3 cases of toilet cleaner, and 86 bottles of Windex. By the time they get to Florida, they're so pooped, they turn around and go home. Believe It? Not! Zwicky was named World Champion Liar of 2000 for his tale in the Burlington, Wisconsin, Liar's Club contest. Sometimes it pays to tell a whopper.

Magnifi-scents

Winners of the annual National Odor-Eaters Rotten Sneaker Contest, held in Montpelier, Vermont, get to have their smelly running shoes enshrined in the Odor-Eaters "Hall of Fumes"!

Cool Designs

Thanks to Ötzi, the ice mummy found in a glacier in the Otzal Alps on the border of Austria and Italy, we now have proof that tattooing began more than 5,300 years ago. Discovered by two hikers in 1991, Ötzi's frozen body had stripes on one ankle, a cross behind one knee, and parallel lines across his back. Scientists surmise that the tattoos, made by rubbing charcoal into cuts, were part of a medical treatment, perhaps used to reduce pain.

Love Me, Love My Couch

In 1998, Elmajean Donnelly of Elwood City, Pennsylvania, beat out 1,200 other contestants in the annual Ugly Couch Contest to win the $2,000 first prize for having the ugliest couch in America!

Good Directions!

A hospital for recovering alcoholics in Paterson, New Jersey, is located at the intersection of Straight and Narrow Streets.

5

AMAZING ESCAPES

Gate Crasher

In November 2004, in an effort to beat a train, 39-year-old Wilbur L. Porter drove around the railroad crossing gates in Deer Park, New York. He was not fast enough. A train going 75 miles per hour struck the back of Porter's sport utility vehicle so hard that the rear door flew off and narrowly missed Bob Weston, who was standing in the lot of his auto repair shop across the street. Weston rushed to the wreck to help the driver — who walked away unharmed! Believe It or Not!

Shaggy Survivors

When hurricane Katrina struck in September 2005, rescuers tended to human victims first, leaving pets to fend for themselves. Luckily, many of them survived, thanks to thousands of volunteers, like David Coupe of Panama City, Florida, who waded through polluted waters to rescue abandoned pets from flooded homes, rooftops, and islands of debris in one of the largest pet rescue efforts in history.

RIPLEY FILE:
7.16.1936

Miraculous Escape!

Two-year-old Dwanna Lee of Eureka, Utah, was struck by a freight train and thrown ten feet through the air. The engine and six cars passed over her body — yet she survived without injury!

Double Trouble

A three-year-old German boy was uninjured after driving the family car 30 feet before crashing it. Four days later, a TV news crew showed up to recreate the scene. They turned their backs for a moment — and the boy drove off again!

Rock-a-byε, Baby

In February 2000, floods engulfed or swept away thousands of homes in Mozambique. To keep from drowning, many families climbed trees. The timing could not have been worse for Sofia Pedro, who was nine months pregnant. Along with her two children and several other people, Pedro spent four days among the branches of a tree before a military helicopter came to rescue them. Imagine the crewman's surprise when he was lowered into the tree and found Pedro had given birth to a baby girl just moments before! Mother, baby, and everyone else in the tree were hoisted into the helicopter and flown to safety.

SHOCK TACTICS

Strokes of Luck

Getting caught outside during a thunderstorm can be dangerous — which is why so many golfers have been struck by lightning. Michael Utley, an amateur golfer, was struck while playing on Cape Cod, Massachusetts, in May 2000. Utley's heart stopped several times. Had his golfing partners not known how to perform CPR, Utley would have died. Since then, Utley has started Struckbylightning.org, an organization devoted to promoting lightning safety and awareness.

**RIPLEY FILE:
9.12.2005**

Shocking Recovery

In 1986, Cliff Meidl was working on a construction site when his jackhammer cut through electrical cables and sent 30,000 volts of electricity through his body. Meidl was badly burned and suffered three heart attacks, but he survived. To avoid having his legs amputated below the knees, he underwent a muscle transplant. Much to everyone's surprise, within three years, Meidl was able to walk again. He then took up kayaking and made the USA Olympic flatwater team — twice!

Rise and Shine! On June 30, 2005, while seven-year-old Kaylee Shriner was sleeping, a bolt of lightning struck her house in Tonganoxie, Kansas, and set her bed on fire. Luckily, Kaylee awoke in the nick of time and jumped out of her flaming bed to safety.

Strike Zone

Weather experts estimate lightning strikes Earth 100 times per second, each time heating the air to a temperature of 50,000 degrees Fahrenheit — five times hotter than the sun's surface!

Live Wire

In 1999, a female black bear showed up on the streets of Albuquerque, New Mexico. Frightened residents called animal control officers, but before they could catch her, the panicked bear climbed up a utility pole, where she was zapped by more than 7,000 volts of electricity and fell 25 feet to the ground. After being airlifted by helicopter to the nearest zoo, the bear was treated and released back into the wild.

GREAT ESCAPES

Anchors "Away"

In June 2002, 62-year-old California resident Richard Van Pham's three-hour pleasure sail to Catalina Island turned into a three-month fight for survival. Van Pham's radio was broken and, after a sudden gale destroyed his mast and threw him off course, he drifted 2,500 miles in the Pacific Ocean. Van Pham sustained himself by eating fish and drinking rainwater. When he was finally rescued almost 300 miles off the coast of Costa Rica, he was grilling a seagull over a fire fueled with wood from his own boat.

**RIPLEY FILE:
4.28.1973**

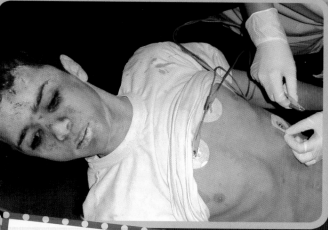

Leap of Faith! Hans Craas and another guide were leading a couple up Switzerland's Piz Palu Mountain. The four climbers were roped together when three of them lost their footing on a ridge and plunged down a crevice. Craas quickly leaped off the opposite side of the ridge and used his weight as a counter-pull on the rope, halting their fall and saving their lives.

Dust Jacket

After their poorly built 11-story apartment building collapsed in February 2004, Ahmet Kalem of Konya, Turkey, was so sure his son was dead that he dug his grave. So when 16-year-old Muhammet was pulled from the rubble the sixth day after the collapse, with just cuts and bruises, his father was overjoyed. Apparently, the concrete dust that covered the boy provided insulation and allowed enough air in to keep him alive, while his sleeping instead of struggling reduced the boy's need for water.

Grrr!

Five-year-old Julius Rosenberg of Winnipeg, Manitoba, plucked his three-year-old sister from the jaws of a black bear — and then growled at the beast until it fled!

"Sweet" Ending

In June 2005, 11-year-old Brennan Hawkins was camping in the Utah mountains with a Boy Scout troop when he wandered off by himself and became hopelessly lost. To keep warm during the cool nights, Brennan slept in a crouching position with his sweatshirt pulled down over his knees. Four days later, he was found, hungry and thirsty but unharmed and in good spirits. When asked how it felt to be on TV, his reply was, "Sweet." Next time, he'll take a compass.

Track Record

A runaway dachshund owned by Tom and Cindy Caruth of Rosemount, Minnesota, survived after being accidentally run over by a train three times in five days. A conductor rescued the pup and returned him to his grateful family. Except for losing part of his tail, the dog was fine.

Waterslide

In 1989, William Lamm of Vero Beach, California, escaped unhurt after being sucked into a water intake pipe and traveling through it for 1,500 feet at 50 miles per hour!

SNAKE*PIT*

On May, 20, 1991, a copperhead slithered out of a vent in the cockpit of a helicopter flying over Rock Hill, South Carolina. The pilot tried to step on the snake, lost control of his helicopter, and crashed into the trees below. The helicopter was destroyed, but the pilot was uninjured. No word about the snake.

S'now Joke!

On December 29, 1993, James and Jennifer Stolpa were traveling with their baby from California to Idaho to visit a sick relative when heavy snow closed Interstate 80. Instead of turning back, the Stolpas took a back road into Nevada, where their truck got stuck in a snowdrift. After five days with only snack food to eat, they left the truck and slogged for miles through waist-high snow before reaching a dead end. Twenty-eight hours later, they found a small cave where they huddled together for warmth. The next day, Jennifer and the baby stayed behind while James left to find help. Almost 48 hours later, he was finally found by a road worker. Rescuers followed James's directions and found Jennifer and the baby. The family had survived eight days of freezing temperatures!

Team Effort

While out on an afternoon hike with her dogs, Michelle Trainor of New Zealand fell 164 feet and was impaled by a tree branch. Grubby and Murdoch, her dogs, retrieved her cell phone, which she used to call for help, and kept her warm until she was rescued.

SQUIRRELLY!

When the lights suddenly go out and you can't use your computer or watch TV, who's to blame? The answer might be squirrels. Areas with large squirrel populations suffer more than their share of blackouts. The furry creatures scurry to the top of telephone poles and squirm into transformers, electrocuting themselves and cutting off power to thousands of people. Now engineers are fitting the vulnerable connections with insulating "boots" that prevent squirrels from coming into contact with live wires.

Give Me a Brake

In February 2004, Angel Eck was driving on Interstate 70 in Denver, Colorado, when her car started accelerating by itself. She tried applying the brakes and downshifting, but nothing worked. Before long, Eck was speeding along at 100 miles per hour, dodging cars and trucks. After 45 minutes of this, she'd traveled about 75 miles. Luckily, by then, the police had been notified about her predicament. A cruiser pulled in front of Eck's car, and the officer slowed until the bumpers were touching and he could bring both cars to a gradual stop. Incredibly, no one was hurt!

Flash Man

Jorge Marquez, a farm worker from Cuba, has been struck by lightning five times in 22 years. The first time was in June 1982, when his hair caught fire and the fillings flew out of his teeth!

6

CRITTER ZONE

BIZARRE BEASTS

Doggone Ugly

In July 2005, a 14-year-old dog named Sam won the World's Ugliest Dog Contest at the Sonoma-Marin Fair in Petaluma, California, for the third year in a row. Sam, a purebred Chinese crested hairless, was considered "un-adoptable" by the folks at the animal shelter when Susie Lockheed rescued him and took him home. After winning the title, Sam made several TV appearances and was scheduled to appear in a show on the ugliest species in the world when, sadly, he died just short of his 15th birthday in November 2005.

**RIPLEY FILE:
1.18.1930**

Flat Leaver! The flying snake of Java, an island in Indonesia, is a rare species that flattens itself out like a ribbon and sails from tree to tree.

E.T., Phone Home

With its huge saucerlike eyes and long, nearly hairless fingers, feet, and tail, the tarsier looks like it could have dropped to Earth from a distant planet. Found only on certain Southeast Asian islands, the rat-size tarsier is actually a primate that sleeps during the day and hunts at night. Like an owl, it can swivel its head nearly 180 degrees in each direction, and suction pads at the ends of its fingers and toes give it a tight grip on any surface.

Fast Food

The star-nosed mole sports the most sensitive nose in the animal kingdom. Composed of 22 fleshy fingerlike rays that squirm in all directions, this talented nose is perfect for tracking mass quantities of insects, worms, and shellfish. These greedy creatures have been clocked downing ten mouthfuls of earthworms in 2.3 seconds, giving new meaning to the phrase "fast food."

Dropping Hints

You can always tell when an Australian wombat has been around by its distinctive cube-shaped droppings.

Ghost Monkeys

Aye-ayes are pretty spooky looking, with their bright green eyes that glow in the dark; large, spoon-shaped ears; twitchy white whiskers; and spindly hands. Perhaps that's why many of the people who share the island of Madagascar with these cat-size primates are afraid of them. A common belief among Malagasies is that aye-ayes bring death to anyone who crosses their path. In some areas, these gentle tree dwellers are killed on sight. However, deforestation is an even greater threat to their survival, making them the world's most endangered primate.

Buzz Off!

Way to Glow!

Even though scorpions live everywhere but Antarctica, scientists once had trouble finding a decent sample to study. That's because scorpions hide in burrows by day and come out to hunt for food only at night. Then scientists discovered that scorpions fluoresce — an elaborate way of saying they glow in the dark — and the problem was solved. Now they can find as many scorpions as they need — just by shining an ultraviolet light near scorpion habitats.

Flash Cards

Ever wonder what causes fireflies to glow? It's bioluminescence, the chemical reaction between oxygen, luciferin, adenosine triphosphate (ATP), and luciferare. Fireflies store the chemicals in their abdomen. When they take in oxygen through the spiracles, or air holes, in their abdomen, they light up. There are about 1,900 species of fireflies, each with a unique flashing code that only others of its species understand.

RIPLEY FILE: 2.03.1961

No Bones About It! The California dogface butterfly's markings are quite unique — on each forewing is a poodle's profile.

Beeware!

Honeybees kill more people each year than do all the poisonous snakes in the world put together.

Going My Way?

Certain beetle species have evolved in ways that really simplify their lives. Take blister beetles, for instance. They lay their eggs on the kind of flowers that bees like best. When the eggs hatch, the larvae wait for the bees to land on a flower so the beetles can latch on to them. The bees unwittingly fly the hungry beetle babies home to hives that are well stocked with beetle food — the eggs and larvae of the bees!

Real Spitfire

In early spring, young froghoppers, also known as spittlebugs, cover themselves with a froth — commonly known as cuckoo spit — that helps them hide from predators. However, that's not the only trick they know. If there were an insect Olympics, the froghopper would be the undisputed winner in the high-jump category. Although it measures a mere two-tenths of one inch, a froghopper can leap to a height of 27 inches. That's pretty astounding when you consider that, to equal the jump, a human would have to clear 650 feet — the height of a 50-story building!

BEASTLY WAYS

Monkey Business

Are baboons born bullies? Scientists studying the animals in Kenya don't think so. A group of baboons, dubbed the Forest Troop, jabbed, kicked, and bit each other on a regular basis. Then the most dominant males contracted tuberculosis while foraging for food in a tourist area. After they died, the rest of the group became more relaxed and affectionate with one another. That was 20 years ago. To this day, the Forest Troop remains kinder and gentler, and new members joining the group mimic their peaceful ways as well.

Gorilla Good-bye

When Babs, a 30-year-old lowland gorilla, died at the Illinois Brookfield Zoo, her caretakers laid her out in the zoo's Tropic World building. Then they opened the doors so that the other gorillas could stream in. Babs's nine-year-old daughter, Bana, lay beside her mother, stroking her fur. Others approached and gently touched her body. One gorilla even held her baby close to Babs, who had lavished the infant with attention. Zoo curator Melinda Pruett Jones explains that, like humans, gorillas have a need to mourn their loved ones and do so naturally in the wild.

RIPLEY FILE: 9.13.1984

Featherbrained!

In an experiment conducted in 1982 by zoologist Malte Andersson of Sweden, male long-tailed widow birds attracted more females when their tail feathers, usually a foot and a half long, were artificially lengthened to two and a half feet.

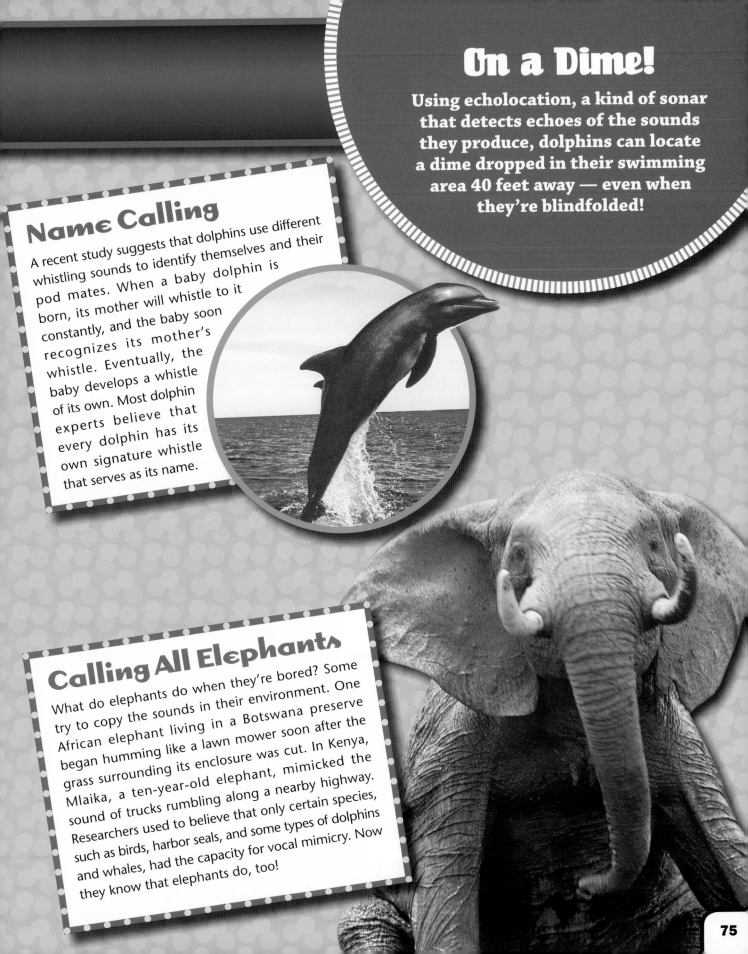

On a Dime!

Using echolocation, a kind of sonar that detects echoes of the sounds they produce, dolphins can locate a dime dropped in their swimming area 40 feet away — even when they're blindfolded!

Name Calling

A recent study suggests that dolphins use different whistling sounds to identify themselves and their pod mates. When a baby dolphin is born, its mother will whistle to it constantly, and the baby soon recognizes its mother's whistle. Eventually, the baby develops a whistle of its own. Most dolphin experts believe that every dolphin has its own signature whistle that serves as its name.

Calling All Elephants

What do elephants do when they're bored? Some try to copy the sounds in their environment. One African elephant living in a Botswana preserve began humming like a lawn mower soon after the grass surrounding its enclosure was cut. In Kenya, Mlaika, a ten-year-old elephant, mimicked the sound of trucks rumbling along a nearby highway. Researchers used to believe that only certain species, such as birds, harbor seals, and some types of dolphins and whales, had the capacity for vocal mimicry. Now they know that elephants do, too!

WILD AND DEADLY

Open Wide

Try not to get too close to a hippopotamus. When one of these enormous beasts opens its mouth wide, it's not a yawn, it's a warning. Their lower canine teeth are actually sharp tusks. The tusks aren't used for chewing; they're used as weapons. These surprisingly fast-moving animals have been known to capsize boats, resulting in the drowning of several occupants.

RIPLEY FILE: 2.28.1999

Shell Shocker! The piddock, a mollusk found along the coasts of Britain and Ireland, should be avoided at all costs. The creature has been known to bore holes right through cast iron. Just imagine what it could do to your hand!

Death by Snail

The marine cone snail has a hollow tooth with a harpoonlike barb at the end. When it detects prey, it sticks out its tooth, called a radula, and uses it to stab, inject paralyzing venom, and reel in its next meal. The cone snail's venom is poisonous enough to kill a human within minutes — yet researchers believe it holds the key to creating a painkiller that's 1,000 times stronger than morphine and has no side effects. Now in clinical testing, the new painkiller may soon be helping thousands of people with arthritis, cancer, and other painful diseases.

Do Not Touch!

South and Central America's tiny poison dart frogs are so beautiful it's hard to imagine just how lethal they can be. However, it takes only 0.0000004 of an ounce of the poison in the skin glands of the most lethal frog to kill an adult human being. Why are they called poison dart frogs? The Chocó people of western Colombia coat the tips of their hunting arrows with the frogs' poison.

Watch the Birdie!

The skin and feathers of the pitohui, a brightly colored songbird of New Guinea, contain the same kind of poison as some types of poison dart frogs!

A Real Mouthful

Imported as pets, Burmese pythons are often abandoned by their owners in Florida's Everglades National Park when they get too big. The snakes grow to be 15 feet long and thrive in this environment. In fact, they're doing so well they may be crowding out other species as well as eating them. The pythons even attack alligators, sometimes with fatal results for both creatures — as in this instance, where the alligator swallowed by the python was so big the snake burst!

CRITTER COMFORT

Heart Strings

Day after day in spring 2002, the heartbreaking cries of Botok, a white bactrian camel, could be heard in the Gobi desert of Mongolia. The newborn had been rejected by his mother. Luckily, the nomadic herding family who owned the camels knew a traditional ritual that might convince the camel to accept her baby. They sent for a violinist, and as he played, the herders stroked the mother's fur and sang to her. When the baby next tried to nurse, the mother nuzzled him tenderly and continued to nurture him.

Friendly Purr-suasion

One day in 2000, Muschi, a small black cat, showed up at the Berlin Zoo in Germany, much to the delight of an Asiatic black bear. The bear, named Mäuschen, even shared her meals of raw meat, dead mice, fruit, and bread with Muschi! In 2004, when Mäuschen was relocated to a cage while her living space was enlarged, Muschi sat outside the cage and mewed until the zookeepers got the message. Now Muschi is back with Mäuschen, cuddling and sharing meals.

Rat-a-cat

In 2005, two white rats made friends with a kitten in Madras, India. The three pals not only play together but also eat and sleep together.

Pen Pals

It's always surprising when a predator and its prey become friends. In the wild, a pig would make a tasty morsel for a tiger. At Thailand's Si Racha Tiger Zoo, instead of eating her piglet pen pals, a Bengal tiger named Saimai clearly enjoys their company. After grooming them with her rough tongue, the young tiger cuddles with the pigs. Perhaps her fondness for the creatures is due to her having been nursed by a sow as a cub.

Gimme Shell-ter

In December 2004, several hippopotamuses living in Kenya were swept out into the Indian Ocean after heavy rains flooded their river home. They all made it back to shore except for one baby, who was spotted in the ocean and rescued. Named Owen, the baby hippo was transported to the Haller Wildlife Park, near Mombasa. There, Owen bonded with a 130-year-old giant tortoise named Mzee, which means "old man" in Swahili. Now Owen follows Mzee everywhere. At naptime, Owen cuddles up close to Mzee and rests his head on the tortoise's shell. Refuge caretakers have witnessed bonding between different mammal species before, but between a reptile and a mammal? This is a first!

EXTRA! EXTRA!

Eeeeeeek!

Scientists estimate that you are never more than 3 feet away from a spider at any given time.

Go Fish!

Alligator snapping turtles can weigh as much as 300 pounds. They require a lot of food, but they're very lazy hunters — which is why the appendage attached to their tongue is so handy. When the turtle is hungry, it lies on the river bottom waiting for a tasty morsel to swim by. Then it opens wide and wriggles its fleshy, wormlike appendage. As soon as a fish takes the "bait," the turtle snaps its jaws down on its meal.

The Better to Hear With

It is easy to distinguish the fennec fox from other types of foxes. Though it weighs in at less than 4 pounds, its huge ears are bigger than those of a rabbit!

Purr-fect Recovery

Besides purring when content, cats also purr when injured. Why is this so? Scientists in London, England, believe they have discovered the answer. A cat's purr is a self-healing tool that helps bones and organs recover from illness and injury. Exposure to similar sound frequencies has been shown to increase bone density in humans.

purrrrrrrrrrrrrrrrrrrrrrrr

That's Batty!

Not much bigger than a bumblebee, the Kitti's hog-nosed bat of Thailand is one of the world's smallest mammals. It is also endangered.

Peek-a-boo!

Amazonian tree ants can capture prey many times larger than themselves. They construct a trap made of fungus and tiny plant hairs, equipped with little holes for the ants to hide in. When a large insect, such as a grasshopper, crawls on the trap, the ants pull on its legs, wings, and antennae so it can't get away. Then worker ants kill the grasshopper by stinging it.

Big Baby

Hercules, a liger living at T.I.G.E.R.S., a Myrtle Beach wildlife sanctuary in South Carolina, is part lion, part tiger. Ligers are the offspring of male lions and female tigers bred in captivity, and are bigger than either of their parents. Standing 10 feet tall on his back legs, Hercules is capable of devouring 100 pounds of meat at a time. At three years old, he tipped the scales at half a ton!

Ferrety Facts

Ferrets have been domesticated since about 3000 BCE — 500 years longer than the house cat. A female ferret is called a jill, and a male is called a hob. A group of ferrets is called a business.

7

SURREAL!

GRAND MUMMIES

Extreme Makeover

Despite the many tomb paintings and sculptures of Tutankhamen, also known as King Tut, scientists continue to wonder what the young pharaoh *really* looked like 3,300 years ago. In 2005, Dr. Zahi Hawass of Egypt's Supreme Council of Antiquities decided to find out. He had 1,700 three-dimensional images, called CT scans, made of Tut's skull and gave them to three teams of forensic artists. Pictured below is the result of the French team's efforts, and at left, a statue of Tut made when he was alive. Which do you think is more accurate?

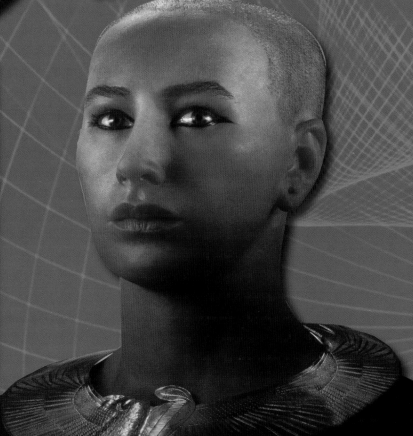

Telltale Heart! Although most internal organs were removed during mummification, the ancient Egyptians would leave the heart inside so it could be weighed in the afterlife as a way of judging a person's worth.

Bad Rap

Lice remains have been found in the wrappings of ancient mummies!

Mummy . . . and Baby

In 1972, hunters stumbled upon eight mummies — six women, a child, and an infant — perfectly preserved by freezing temperatures. The 500-year-old mummies were in a cave in Qilakitsoq, Greenland. How they died is uncertain, but CT scans indicate that the baby was buried alive. Why? Perhaps because the Inuit once believed that if a mother died, her baby should be buried with her so that they could travel together to the land of the dead.

Grand Opening

In 1993, Russian archaeologist Natalia Polosmak uncovered a wooden tomb high on the Ukok Plateau in Siberia. Above the burial chamber were the skeletons of six horses. After opening the carved wooden coffin, Polosmak had to wait for the ice inside to melt before she could view the contents: a tattooed woman wearing an elaborate headdress and fine clothing. A member of the Pazyryk people, the "Ice Maiden" was buried more than 2,400 years ago. Archaeologists believe she was probably a priestess.

DEM BONES

Boneyard

Every 20 years at a cemetery in Chacheonsao, Thailand, hundreds of skeletons are dug up to provide space for new burials. Believing their work will bring them great merit, Buddhist volunteers clean the skeletons, which are then dried and reassembled for cremation.

Brain Teaser

In 1995, *La Belle*, a ship belonging to French explorer René-Robert Cavalier, Sieur de la Salle (1643–1687), was discovered off the coast of Texas. As archaeologists went through the ship, which sank in 1686, they found a complete human skeleton. It was so well preserved that a large part of the brain still remained in the skull! CT scans were used to make replicas of the skull, and a facial reconstruction was completed that, along with DNA tests, may help identify the crewman. Meanwhile, his remains are buried at the Texas State Cemetery in Austin.

RIPLEY FILE:
7.19.1978

Pedi-care! The mummified feet of wealthy Egyptians were often preserved in special cases on which were modeled accurate replicas of their sandaled feet.

Mystery Lake

In 1942, melting snow revealed hundreds of 1,500-year-old skeletons strewn along the shores of India's Roopkund Lake, high in the Himalayas. How the people died was a mystery until 2005, when researchers concluded they were killed by giant hailstones.

Out of Fashion

If you don't mind looking at dead bodies, you might find the catacombs under a Capuchin monastery in Palermo, Italy, the perfect place to see how people dressed throughout history. Beginning in 1599 and ending in 1920, thousands of dressed-up, dried-out corpses have been hung on hooks, laid out on shelves, or tucked into coffins. Since gravity has distorted their facial features, many of them appear to be screaming. It would be hard to find a spookier fashion show!

1799 — A Grave Fear

George Washington was not afraid of dying, but he was afraid of being buried alive — a fear that was quite widespread before embalming became common practice. Less than an hour before he died on December 14, Washington told his secretary, "Do not let my body be put into the vault less than two days after I am dead."

1826 — Dead Heat

John Adams (below) and Thomas Jefferson, the second and third presidents of the United States, shared a friendly rivalry all their lives. Minutes before he died, John Adams sat up in his bed and whispered, "Jefferson survives," unaware that Jefferson, too, had died that same morning — July 4 — 50 years to the day after the signing of the Declaration of Independence!

1865 — Train of Death

Abraham Lincoln's funeral train passed through more than 400 towns and cities on its 20-day journey from Washington, D.C., to Springfield, Illinois, a distance of 1,654 miles. Along the way, at least a dozen funerals were held for the assassinated president.

1881 — Bad Medicine

On July 2, James Garfield was shot, but he died because of medical incompetence. Sixteen doctors poked around in his body, trying unsuccessfully to find the bullet, without having washed their hands or sterilized their instruments. On September 19, Garfield, his heart probably weakened by more than two months of infection, died of a heart attack.

1841 — Long and Short

On March 4, William Henry Harrison took almost two hours to deliver his 8,445-word inaugural speech, the longest on record. It was a cold, nasty day, but Harrison wore no overcoat, hat, or gloves, and he caught a severe cold that turned into pneumonia. He died exactly one month later, after having served the shortest presidential term on record.

1845 — Potty Mouth

Known as a champion of the common man, Andrew Jackson died on June 8 from heart failure. His pet parrot was allowed to attend the funeral but had to be removed because it wouldn't stop cursing!

1850 — Rumor Had It

Zachary Taylor was the second president to die in office, but he is the only president to have been exhumed. Rumors that he was poisoned persisted until he was dug up in 1991 and tests proved the theories were false. The real cause of death, however, remains unknown.

1848 — Outsized

The coffin chosen for John Quincy Adams was so big that it would not fit into the vault. So his funeral had to be stopped for stonemasons to make the vault wider.

1963 — Deadly Coincidence

John F. Kennedy was assassinated on November 22. Lee Harvey Oswald shot Kennedy from a warehouse and was found in a theater. John Wilkes Booth assassinated Abraham Lincoln in a theater and was found in a warehouse.

SERIOUSLY GROSS

Pop Go the Toads

In 2005, something unnatural was happening to the toads in Hamburg, Germany: They were croaking, but not in a good way. One after another, the creatures were swelling up more than three times their normal size — and then exploding! Scientists didn't know what to make of it until one of them observed that crows were pecking out the toads' livers, leaving gaping holes in their chests. As a defense, the toads puffed themselves up. Air filled the chest holes, their lungs burst, and nothing was left but a gooey mess. Frogs' legs, anyone?

Creatures Were Stirring!

On December 6, 2004, Merida, the capital of Yucatan, Mexico, resembled an Alfred Hitchcock movie as swarms of locusts swept through. Stores were decked out with bows and ornaments for the holidays, but instead of shoppers, the streets were crammed with large, crunchy pests; the voices of carolers were replaced with a high-pitched buzz; and instead of snow, the air was filled with insects!

Creepy-Crawly House

Home is where the heart is — and some other things, too!

BATHROOM
You may think the bathroom counter is a good place to keep your toothbrush, but you would be wrong. One flush of the toilet and up comes a spray of bacteria-filled water droplets. What goes up must come down, and some of the bacteria are bound to settle on — you guessed it — your toothbrush.

KITCHEN
Compared to the bathroom, the kitchen must be pretty clean, right? Think again! Random testing shows that most kitchens are contaminated with fecal bacteria from raw meat. In fact, the sponges used to wipe down the counters and wash the dishes have far more germs than a toilet seat — unless you live in a vegetarian household, that is.

LIVING ROOM
Don't touch that telephone! It's covered in germs. For that matter, so are your computer mouse, your handheld video game, and your TV remote. Many of the germs are probably of the rhinovirus kind, left there by those who don't wash their hands after coughing or sneezing.

DINING ROOM
Next time your parents ask you to vacuum up the crumbs after dinner, tell them about this: A vacuum cleaner is one of the best ways ever invented to spread dust mite fecal pellets. The pellets are so tiny that they are easily sucked between the fibers of vacuum cleaner bags and escape the same way, as well as through the vacuum cleaner's exhaust.

BEDROOM
Think you're safe in the bedroom? You are if you don't mind sharing your sleeping space with millions of dust mites! You can't see them, but they're there, eating flakes of dead skin shed by you and your family, pooping, and multiplying! Each dust mite creates up to 20 pellets of microscopic waste a day. *Achoo!*

91

Min-imum Min-ute Hand

When Queen Min of Korea was killed and her body burned by Japanese assassins in 1895, the bone of one little finger was all the Koreans could find. An ancient section of Seoul was then destroyed to make a beautiful burial ground for her finger. In May 2005, descendants of two of the assassins traveled there to apologize and beg forgiveness for their ancestors' crime.

Leave a Message

The grave of Guy Akrish of Ashkelon, Israel, who died at age 17 in a traffic accident in 1998, has a headstone shaped like a giant cell phone. The epitaph reads, "Hello, this is Guy. How are you doing?"

Going Out with a Bang!

Celebrate Life, a company in California, will scatter a deceased person's ashes in a spectacular fireworks display called Heaven Sent. Themes include "Knocking on Heaven's Door," "Stairway to Heaven," and "When Irish Eyes Are Smiling."

Look Ma, No Hands!

Since Swiss inventor Juerg Lumpert invented his disinfecting element, cleaning the toilet has never been easier. You don't even need soap! Using ultraviolet light, the invention hovers over the toilet seat, ridding it of germs without using detergents.

Blowing His Own Horn

Because of a shortage of bugle players, a recording of USA Army Sergeant Major Woodrow "Woody" English playing "Taps" has been copied onto digital chips that were then fitted to electronic bugles used at military funerals around the country. A flip of the switch, and the bugle plays by itself. English believes he'll be the first bugler ever to play at his own funeral!

Dying for Business

That's the slogan at Skeletons in the Closet, a gift shop in the Los Angeles Coroner's Office. There, customers can buy hats, mugs, clothing, body bags, toe tags, beach towels, mouse pads, key chains, and magnets — all appropriately decorated with skeletons, skulls, and body outlines.

Dead Beats

In Madagascar, an island off the coast of Africa, many people believe that honoring their dead loved ones with a sumptuous feast will bring the entire family good fortune. Every five years or so, families observe a holiday called Famadihana, when they remove their dead relatives from their tombs, fill them in on family gossip, and even dance with them. Afterward, the corpses are given new shrouds and returned to their graves.

Doggone!

Cemeteries aren't just for deceased *people*. More than 600 pet cemeteries in the USA provide a place for people to memorialize their beloved pets. The oldest one still active is the Hartsdale Pet Cemetery in New York, which was established in 1896. Almost 70,000 pets are buried there.

8

BODILY ODDITIES

Smart Bandages

Researchers at the University of Rochester in New York are perfecting bandages that indicate if an infection is present. Layers of silicon in the bandages contain molecules that bind with certain types of bacteria, such as *E. coli* and strep. Using a handheld device, health care workers can examine the bandage with laser light. Depending on what color the bandage turns, they'll know what kind of bacteria is in the wound.

RIPLEY FILE:
11.09.2004

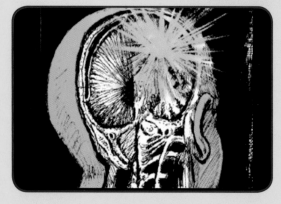

Mind Control! In 2001, Matthew Nagle of Massachusetts was stabbed and his spinal cord severed, leaving him paralyzed from the neck down. Now, an experimental device implanted in his brain allows him to play computer games by translating thoughts into movements.

Seeing with Sound

Imagine being blind for years and then suddenly being able to see again. Thanks to revolutionary software called vOICe, a blind person can wear glasses or a headset fitted with a camera and earphones to "see." The vOICe system (OIC stands for "Oh, I see!") was developed by Dr. Peter Meijer of The Netherlands to convert camera images into soundscapes. For example, a bright spot of light to a person's left will produce a short beep on the left. If it comes closer, the tone of the beep will rise. Working together, the various sounds allow a person to create a mental image of his or her surroundings.

Auto Pilot

In 2004, Professor Thomas DeMarse at the University of Florida used rat neurons to grow a living brain in a dish. The brain can sense and control airplane movements on a flight simulator!

Minding the Store

In 2003, P. Read Montague, a neuroscientist at Baylor College of Medicine in Houston, Texas, discovered that taste isn't the only consideration when people choose a soft drink. In a blind taste test, more people preferred Pepsi, but when they were told they were drinking Coke, Coke was the winner hands down. According to brain scans, tasting stimulated the part of the brain associated with rewards. However, when the brand name came into play, the part associated with self-image was also activated. Now "neuromarketers" are hoping to use brain scans to determine which products are most likely to trigger the magic words, "I'll buy it!"

Trust Me!

A team of researchers at the University of Zurich, Switzerland, has shown that oxytocin, a hormone produced by new mothers, can make people more trusting. In an experiment, some of the subjects were asked to inhale oxytocin, while others inhaled a placebo. Afterward, the subjects played a game that involved investing their money. The results? Those who inhaled the oxytocin were twice as likely as the others to risk all their money! Is it any surprise that there's already a body spray called Liquid Trust?

CRAZY CURES

Rock-a-bye Babies

For several years, newborn babies at Kosice-Saca Hospital in Slovakia have been wearing headphones. Why? The doctors feel that the next best thing to the comfort of hearing a mother's heartbeat around the clock are the soft sounds of music by Mozart and Vivaldi. The music helps to relieve not only the babies' stress but also the nurses'!

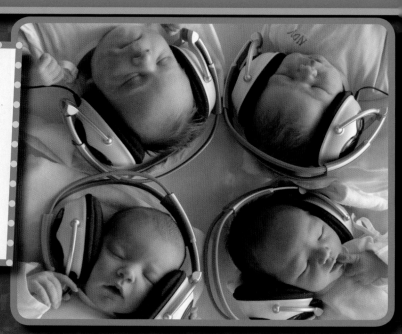

RIPLEY FILE:
11.09.2004

Ribbit-ing Glue! Michael Tyler of Adelaide University in Australia discovered that two types of Australian burrowing frogs secrete a sticky substance from their skin that traps insects. In 2004, he used the stuff on sheep to hold together torn knee cartilage until it healed. It worked on the sheep, and next, doctors plan to try it on humans with knee injuries.

Ray of Hope

When photosensitized cancer cells are zapped with laser light, the cells release a chemical that kills them. Unfortunately, the light doesn't penetrate far enough to reach most cancers. In 2003, a group of scientists at University College London tried something new. In the laboratory, they inserted the firefly gene responsible for producing the enzyme luciferace into cancer cells. After making the cells sensitive to light, they added the protein called luciferin. Together, the luciferace and luciferin caused the cells to light up like fireflies — which killed 89 percent of them.

Kernel of Truth

Centuries ago, the Maya used their own version of penicillin to treat ulcers and some types of infections — mold called cuxum, which grew on roasted corn that had been left to rot!

Mice on Ice

Mark Roth, a scientist at the Fred Hutchinson Cancer Research Center in Seattle, Washington, seems to have found the key to inducing a state of suspended animation. In 2005, he and his team of researchers exposed six mice to air that contained a small amount of hydrogen sulfide. Within a few hours, the mice's metabolism had slowed by 90 percent. When the mice were revived, tests showed they were functioning normally. If these results can be duplicated in humans, the method could be used on people waiting for an organ transplant or to help prevent additional damage after a stroke or heart attack.

INSIDE OUT

Brain

The Milky Way galaxy has about 100 billion stars — about the same number of cells that are in your brain.

Nose
When exposed to the sun or other very bright lights, about 25 percent of all people sneeze. It's called Autosomal Dominan Compelling Helio-Ophthalmic Outburst syndrome — or ACHOO for short.

Hair
Using microscopic examination and DNA testing, forensic scientists can tell a person's age, gender, and race from a single strand of the person's hair.

Teeth
The only natural substance that is harder than your tooth enamel is a diamond!

Kidneys
Your kidneys filter about 50 gallons of fluid every day.

Liver

The liver is the the the only organ that can regenerate itself. If two-thirds of the liver is surgically removed, it will be back to its normal size in about a week.

Bones

There are 206 bones in your body — and together, your hands and feet account for 106 of them.

Skin

A typical human grows a complete new skin about 1,000 times in a lifetime. Most dust particles in a house are flakes of shed human skin.

Heart

Every year, your heart beats about 38 million times, pumping about 700,000 gallons of blood.

Blood Vessels

If all your blood vessels were straightened out and joined together, they would measure about 60,000 miles long.

What Are the Odds?

**RIPLEY FILE:
9.26.2005**

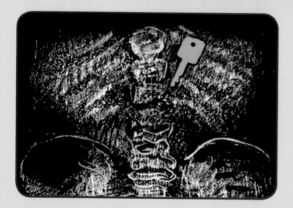

Skeleton Key! While playing a prank in June 2005, Arthur Richardson of Denver, Nebraska, accidentally swallowed the key to his friend's new truck. Since it would be some time before it came out naturally, they took Richardson's X ray to locksmith John Somers, who used it to create a new key — and it worked!

Thumbs Up

John Evans of Springfield, Illinois, suffered severe injuries when he was struck by a train. He woke up to discover he'd needed transfer surgery — that is, his left hand had to be attached to his right arm so he'd at least have one working limb!

Headstrong

In 1997, Alison Kennedy was riding on a train in England when a stranger plunged a 6-inch knife hilt-deep into her skull — yet Kennedy survived the attack with only minor aftereffects!

I Say, Old Chap!

When Judi Roberts of Sarasota, Florida, recovered her voice after having suffered a stroke in 1999, she began speaking with a British accent. Some people thought she was faking it, but in 2003, doctors finally diagnosed her with "foreign accent syndrome." Though extremely rare, there have been other cases of head trauma patients waking up speaking with Polish, German, British, Spanish, Scandinavian, Asian, French, Slavic, Hungarian, and Irish accents they'd never had before!

Twinsets

Nicky Owen of Leeds, England, has an identical twin sister. In 1996, Owen gave birth to identical twin boys. Seven years later, she again had twin boys, this time nonidentical. What are the odds of this happening? About 11 million to one!

Larger Than Life

The only time Walter Hudson of Hempstead, New York, ever went near a scale, he weighed 1,197 pounds. Though he spent the last 27 years of his life in his bedroom, he did not lack for companionship. His good humor and gentle ways made him a favorite of his many nieces and nephews — and despite his weight, he was healthy. In 1987, Hudson became famous when he got stuck in his bedroom doorway, and it took eight firefighters three hours to rescue him. Soon he was beset by people who encouraged him to lose weight with one fad diet or another. After several years of dieting, Hudson's health deteriorated, and he died in 1991.

**RIPLEY FILE:
9.29.2005**

Touching Performance! Nate Richard of Homosassa, Florida, can perform the very unusual act of touching his elbow with his four-inch-long tongue.

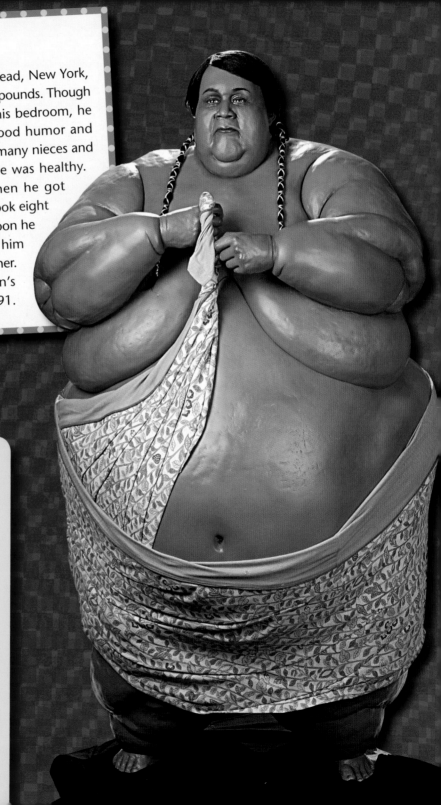

Entailed

A child named Balaji, born in 2001, is being worshipped by his community in India because he was born with a tail!

Stubble Trouble

Grace Gilbert of Kalkaska County, Michigan, traveled with the Ringling Brothers and Barnum and Bailey Circus during the early 20th century. Why did people stand in line to see her? She had a beard — *and* it was 10 inches long!

Towering Spirit

Weighing 7.5 pounds at birth, Ella Ewing (1872–1913) of Gorin, Missouri, seemed perfectly normal, but by age 14, she was already 6 feet 2 inches tall. Ewing finally reached her full height at age 22 — 8 feet 4 inches! Because standard 8-foot ceilings were too low for her, she had to duck to walk through the family house, and kneel to look out a window. People stared at Ewing wherever she went, so she decided she might as well get paid for it and joined the Barnum and Bailey Circus. She used her earnings to build herself the perfect home. It had 10-foot ceilings and custom-made furniture, including a bed that was 9 feet long.

Giggle Cure

The late Norman Cousins believed that a laugh a day would keep the doctor away. In 1964, hospitalized with a severe disease called ankylosing spondylitis, Cousins was in so much pain, he could barely move. Given a poor chance of recovery, he decided to cure himself. Cousins left the hospital, took massive doses of vitamin C (under the guidance of his family doctor), and tried controlling his pain by watching funny TV shows and movies that made him laugh. It worked! Cousins recovered and lived another 26 years!

Cool!

In 2001, Dr. Birgit Schittek and her colleagues at Eberhard-Karls University in Tubingen, Germany, discovered a germ-killing protein in sweat and isolated the gene responsible for it. Both gene and protein are called dermicidin. The protein is manufactured in the sweat glands and helps fight infections from a fungus and several types of bacteria, including *E. coli*.

Brain Trust

Eight human brains are displayed in a glass case on the second floor of the psychology department at Cornell University in Ithaca, New York. They're part of a collection that once contained 600 brains begun in 1889 by Professor Bert Green Wilder. Wilder collected the brains of dead scholars, co-workers, friends, and criminals. About 200 remained in 1978, but many were badly deteriorated and had to be discarded. Today, there are only about 70 brains — including Wilder's. Most are stored in a closet.

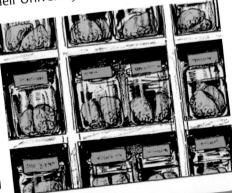

Slick!

In 2004, an elevator company drained hydraulic fluid into drums and left them in the parking lot of a hospital in North Carolina. The barrels were labeled MON-KLENZ, the name of a detergent used to wash surgical tools, so hospital workers called the detergent supplier to pick them up. The supplier, unaware of what was really in the drums, put them in a warehouse and, later, shipped the drums back out as detergent. The result? About 3,800 patients at two hospitals in the Duke University Health System were operated on with surgical instruments that had been cleaned with hydraulic fluid instead of detergent! Oops!

Self-Surgery

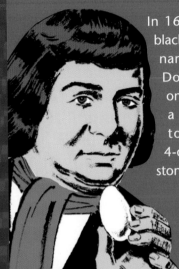

In 1651, a Dutch blacksmith by the name of Jan de Doot operated on himself with a kitchen knife to remove a 4-ounce kidney stone!

Small Versifier

As a child, English poet Alexander Pope (1688–1744) had poor health and suffered from Pott's disease, a type of tuberculosis that causes a curvature of the spine. As a result, he never grew taller than 4 feet 6 inches and had to wear a corset as a body brace to prop himself up.

Soap Story

Founded in 1858, the Mütter Museum at the College of Physicians in Philadelphia, Pennsylvania, holds more than 20,000 items. Among them are a giant colon and the shared liver of conjoined twins Chang and Eng, who lived during the early 1800s. One of the strangest items, however, is the body of a woman who was buried in soil that turned her corpse into soap!

9

Psych!

HEAD SPINNERS

Ghost Town

In Lily Dale, New York, you don't need letters, e-mail, or phone calls to get a message from a loved one — especially if that loved one happens to be dead! Founded in 1879, the town is home to the largest community of spiritualists in the world, many of whom are also psychics. Visitors can attend free public readings by mediums at Inspiration Stump, located in a forest clearing. For private readings, donations start at $40. However, clients not satisfied with the services of a registered Lily Dale Assembly medium can apply to the organization for a full refund.

Star Crossed! Russian astrologer Marina Bai sued NASA for the equivalent of about $300 million, claiming that the Deep Impact missile, which crashed into comet Tempel 1, had upset the balance of the universe, thereby interfering with her work and altering her horoscope. The case was dismissed by a Moscow court in November 2005, but Bai's lawyer planned to appeal.

Spooky!

If you're afraid of ghosts, stay away from Prestbury in Gloucestershire: It's said to be the most haunted village in England. Among the spirits spotted there, are a knight in armor, a shepherd and his sheep, and the Black Abbot, who haunts the churchyard. When photographer Derek Stafford developed some pictures he'd taken in the floodlit churchyard on November 22, 1990, he found a ghostly hooded figure, assumed to be the Abbot, looming over the gravestones!

Ghost Writer

In 1998, three workers at a museum near Havana, Cuba, quit their jobs after they reported seeing the ghost of writer Ernest Hemingway.

Golden Girl

On March 5, 1986, a metallic "mask" appeared on the face of a psychic called Katie. According to Dr. Berthold E. Schwarz, a retired psychiatrist and researcher in psychic phenomena, Katie's masks begin as tiny dots of glittery gold on her face and spread to other parts of her body. When metal specimens from her face, chest, and arms were tested, one turned out to be gold, and another 98 percent copper and 2 percent zinc. Is there something in Katie's physical makeup that causes these outbreaks or is she somehow faking it? No one really knows.

WHEEL OF FORTUNE

What Goes Around

After a woman returned $11,000 worth of money she found on a street in Haarlem, The Netherlands, in 1999, she won the equivalent of $41,900 in the Dutch lottery.

A Prize for the Age

In 1797, George Mitford let his daughter, English novelist Mary Russell Mitford (1787–1865), pick the number for a ticket in the Irish lottery for her tenth birthday. She picked 2224 because the numbers added up to ten. Her father bought her the ticket — and Mary won first prize: £20,000 — the equivalent of about $88,800!

Pennies from Heaven

In 1976, two German clergymen encountered a veritable windfall when the equivalent of $1,130 worth of bills floated down from the sky.

Going by the Numbers

In 2004, 70 bidders in China competed in an online auction for the cell phone number 135 8585 8585, which sounds like "Let me be rich be rich be rich be rich" in Chinese. The highest bid was 9 million yuan — the equivalent of $1,100,000!

Found Art

In 1998, Wanda Bell, an antique collector from Nashville, Tennessee, bought a painting for $25. Underneath it was a rare portrait by artist Sheldon Peck (1797–1868) titled *Gentleman with Red Sash* — which was valued at $250,000!

Cat-call

Linda McManamon of Galveston, Texas, won $3,700,000 in a lottery using numbers she says were picked by her pet cat.

Beating the Odds

Donna Goeppert of Bethlehem, Pennsylvania, must have been born under a lucky star. In January 2005, she won $1,000,000 with a scratch-off lottery ticket. In June 2005, she bought another lottery ticket and won another $1,000,000! The odds? According to the lottery, to win just once, the odds are 1.44 million to 1. According to a Lehigh University professor, to win twice after buying 100 tickets, the odds are 419 million to 1!

CHANCES ARE

RIPLEY FILE:
3.26.1945

Happy Anniversary! In 1943, during World War II, Master Sergeant John Hassebrock of Buffalo Center, Iowa, married a Women's Army Corps corporal before leaving for Europe. In the confusion of war, the couple lost track of each other. Then one evening, when Hassebrock was spending the night at a farmhouse near the front lines in France, he ran into his wife — on the exact date and hour of their first wedding anniversary!

Dream-scapes

For more than 20 years, David Mandell of Great Britain has used watercolors to paint his dreams. Then he takes the paintings downtown and has himself photographed holding them beneath the bank's electronic clock, which shows the date. Why does he go to such great lengths? It seems a number of his dreams have come true, and Mandell wants proof that the dreams occurred before the actual events take place. Among his most memorable dreams are those that anticipated the sarin gas attack on a subway in Tokyo, Japan, in 1995 and the Twin Towers tragedy in New York City in 2001!

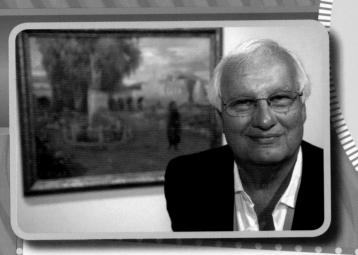

White buffalo are considered sacred by the Lakota Sioux, but according to the National Bison Association, the chances of one being born are only one in ten million — yet since 1997, seven white buffalo have been born at the Spirit Mountain Ranch in Flagstaff, Arizona!

Windfall by a Landslide

Along with others in his Laguna Beach, California, neighborhood, 74-year-old Albert Trevino's $1.8 million house was badly damaged in a landslide in 2005. Afterward, homeowners were given 15 minutes in their teetering homes to gather keepsakes and valuables. Trevino's son grabbed a painting — one that his Dad had bought 20 years earlier at a yard sale for less than $100. An artist who saw the painting recognized the signature as that of Joseph Kleitsch, a noted California Impressionist from the 1920s. A dealer estimates the painting could fetch up to $500,000!

ESP: Extremely Smart Parrot!

In 1997, Aimée Morgana of New York City began teaching her African grey parrot, N'kisi, to speak. By age five, he had a vocabulary of more than 700 words and could speak in grammatically correct sentences. N'kisi also seems to have a bit of ESP. In a controlled experiment, Morgana and N'kisi were put in separate rooms and filmed as Morgana opened envelopes containing picture cards. The parrot used so many appropriate words to describe the pictures that the odds against his doing so by chance were about 2,000 to 1!

115

IT'S ALL AN ILLUSION!

❶ Color Theory

Which red diamonds in the figure are darker?

❷ Two for One

In 1915, a cartoonist named W. E. Hill adapted the picture above from a trading card. Do you see a young woman or an old woman?

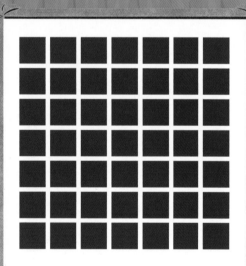

❸ Seeing Things

Are there pale circles between the squares? What happens when you try to look directly at them?

❹ Getting It Started

Are the tiles in the picture uneven? Test them with a ruler.

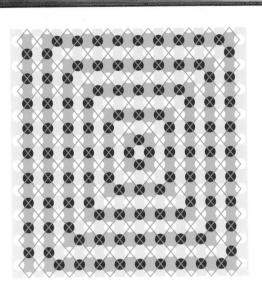

⑤ Mind-Bending

Do the orange lines in the picture look curved?

⑥ Keeping Your Distance

Is the top hat higher than it is wide at the brim?

⑦ Staying in Shape

Not counting the diamond, what shape do you first notice in the figure? Can you see another shape?

⑧ Easy Reading

Tilt the page down and away from you. Can you see the letters? What do they say?

Red Hot!

When it comes to winning, athletes might do well to consider a 2004 British study which found that wearing the color red gives competitors a bit of an edge. It seems that when equally matched Olympians were paired in one-on-one events, such as freestyle wrestling, those who were randomly assigned red outfits won their competitions about 55 percent of the time compared to their blue-clad opponents, who won just 45 percent of the time.

Down Will Come Baby

On August 28, 1947, a two-year-old baby fell out of a second-story window in Roxbury, Massachusetts — and was caught by 12-year-old James Carew. Both children were uninjured!

Medium Success

Business astrologers make predictions based on when and where a company was incorporated.

Holy Moley!

Moleosophy is the art of divining a person's destiny by studying the moles on his or her body!

The Die Is Cast

In 1066, an astrologer assured William the Conqueror that when he invaded England with 900 ships, he would meet with no resistance. The prediction came true, but William wasn't terribly impressed. It seems that two overloaded ships went down with all hands lost — including the astrologer — and William thought a man would be a fool to listen to a prophet who could not foretell his own fate!

Pieces of Eight

After Hurricane Jeanne swept through Florida in September 2004, marine archaeologist Joel Ruth took a walk on a beach in Brevard County and found 180 Spanish silver coins dating back nearly 300 years, which had washed ashore from a shipwreck. Their value was estimated at $40,000!

Haunted Car

The engine of a van owned by Kevin Wise of New Philadelphia, Ohio, miraculously turned itself on six minutes after firefighters had extinguished a fire under its hood.

Luck of the Irish

On May 3, 1972, Patrick Donnelly of Belfast, Ireland, stopped to pick up a wallet he saw lying in the road. In order to find the name of its owner, Donnelly leafed through the wallet only to discover that the owner's name was — Patrick Donnelly! The first Patrick Donnelly contacted the second, who lived in the nearby town of Augher, and returned the lost wallet.

10

THIS AND THAT

Making a Spectacle

The MicroOptical Corporation makes electronic eyewear that can be plugged in to various devices, allowing wearers to see an image floating in space just in front of their eyes. Currently, the eyewear is being used in industry, medicine, and law enforcement. For example, surgeons can use the eyewear to check their patients' vital signs without having to turn away from what they're doing. Before long, the eyewear will be available for consumers to plug in and check e-mail, surf the Web, watch a movie, and more.

RIPLEY FILE: 1.30.2004

Lost and Found! In 2003, Stratech Systems of Singapore introduced Parkvasive, a surveillance system that helps owners find the exact location of a car in a parking lot when they can't remember where they left it.

Pumped!

A kids' merry-go-round in South Africa can be much more than child's play. The ride, manufactured by a company called Roundabout Outdoor, is connected to a water pump. As the children spin around and around, the merry-go-round pumps water from a well — as much as 370 gallons per hour. In remote areas, it's not uncommon for women and children to spend six hours every day carrying water for long distances. With a play pump in their village, they won't have to.

Wired!

An interactive Cinderella comforter made by WestPoint Home is woven from conductive threads that when touched, light up and make a *swoosh* sound as though a fairy godmother has just waved her wand — exactly what every child needs to get to sleep!

Splish Splash

The Dolphin Watercraft, a one-person submersible built by Innespace Productions, not only looks like its namesake but also performs like it. The boat buzzes along the surface, dives as deep as three feet, "flies" underwater, and pops back up with a series of twists and flips.

Spin Factor

In 2005, the Nissan Motor Company unveiled a new concept car called the Pivo. Described as a "rotating egg on wheels," the Pivo has a three-seat cabin that can pivot 360 degrees, doing away with the need to reverse. That maneuverability, coupled with its 9-foot length, makes the Pivo a breeze to parallel park, even in tight spaces. Other innovations include a display screen that runs along the bottom of the windshield, a monitor that eliminates blind spots, and a zero-emissions electric motor.

RIPLEY FILE:
10.30.2004

Auto-graph, Anyone?

As celebrity cars go, the original Batmobile, built in 1966 for the TV show starring Adam West, has to be one of the most famous. So would you believe that George Barris was asked to design and build a fabulous fantasy car — and to complete it in just three weeks? To save time, Barris modified a 19-foot-long Lincoln Futura that he bought for $1. He replaced the engine, added flashing lights, fashioned bat "ears" around the headlights, and created a hood-ornament "nose" and chain cutter. The Futura's long fins, of course, doubled as bat wings.

Toolin' Around! The Dolmar company of Hamburg, Germany, has put together a 170-horsepower motorcycle, called the Dolmette, which is powered by 24 gas-driven chain saws!

Smart Car

A Japanese company has invented a two-seated vehicle that uses optical sensors to measure and analyze traffic signs and road conditions!

Hot Cars

Tuners are hobbyists who spend considerable time and money adding pricey gear to ho-hum cars. After they've turned their "ugly ducklings" into swans, tuners get to show off their customized creations at Hot Import Nights, America's traveling tuner car show. Les Wong, a dentist from Lodi, California, often draws large crowds with his bright red 1993 Mazda RX-7 all decked out with $100,000 worth of equipment, including custom etched glass, m1 installed wide body kit, camouflage paint scheme, racing seats, and Endless big brake kit.

FASTER, FASTER!

START

1898

The first car race, held on December 18 at Achères, France, was called "wheel racing" because it was the first time a race was held where only gear-powered vehicles were eligible. The winner was Count Gaston de Chasseloup-Laubat who achieved the record-breaking speed of 39.244 miles per hour in his Jeantaud, an electric car.

1927

The Napier-Campbell Bluebird (below) was the first car designed specifically to break the land speed record. On February 4, Malcolm Campbell drove the gasoline-powered car at a record speed of 174.88 miles per hour at Pendine Sands, Wales. At Daytona Beach, Florida, on March 29, Henry Segrave reached a velocity of 203.792 miles per hour in a Sunbeam 1000 HP and became the first driver to exceed 200 miles per hour.

FINISH

1997

On September 25, Andy Green drove the Thrust SSC II, powered by two jet engines, at a speed of 714.144 miles per hour, becoming the first driver to exceed 700 miles per hour. On October 15, he drove the same car at a speed of 763.035 and became the first driver to break the sound barrier — also known as Mach 1 — which is 1.021 times the speed that sound travels through air!

1970

Gary Gabelech set a new land speed record of 622.407 miles per hour in the Blue Flame, the first rocket-powered car, on October 23.

THE BLUE FLAME

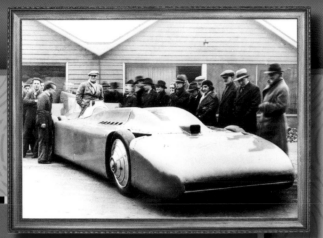

1935

On September 3, Malcolm Campbell set another record when he became the first driver to exceed 300 miles per hour. He drove a Campbell Railton Rolls-Royce Bluebird at 301.129 miles per hour.

1963

On August 5, Craig Breedlove drove the Spirit of America, the first car to be powered by a jet engine, at a speed of 407.518 miles per hour at Utah's Bonneville Salt Flats. He was the first driver to break 400 miles per hour.

1965

On November 15, Craig Breedlove set yet another record when he drove a jet-powered racecar called the Spirit of America Sonic 1 at 600.601 miles per hour at the Bonneville Salt Flats, becoming the first driver to go faster than 600 miles per hour on land.

1964

Craig Breedlove also became the first driver to exceed 500 miles per hour, when he drove the same jet-powered Spirit of America at 526.277 miles per hour at the Bonneville Salt Flats on October 15.

EXTREME FASHION

Chipping Away! Created by Adidas, the Adidas 1 running shoe uses a built-in microprocessor to adjust to a jogger's running style and to changes in terrain.

Sizing You Up

Do you hate trying on clothes? Well, if a company called Intellifit has its way, dressing rooms will soon become a thing of the past. You'll simply step into a glass enclosure and wait about ten seconds while a scanner collects information from about 200,000 data points on your body. When you emerge, a paper reading will pop out giving the sizes that will fit you best in different brands. The service is free — except for customer age ranges, sizes, and other marketing information, which is collected for the brands that pay for this service.

Thinking Outside the Bag

Build Your Own Bag (bYOB), created by Gauri Nanda at the Massachusetts Institute of Technology, is a network of modular fabric "blocks" with tiny built-in sensors, conductive Velcro patches, and a voice synthesizer, which can be added to your handbag. As soon as you pick up your bag, it will remind you if you've forgotten something important, like keys or your wallet, and light up when opened in the dark.

Sweet!

Forget your deodorant? You won't have to worry if you wear clothing from a company named Hot Chillys, which features fabric woven with Bio-Silver, an antimicrobial fiber that does away with BO.

Invisible Man

Though Kazutoshi Obana may look like he's invisible, he's really demonstrating optical camouflage technology at Tokyo University. A video camera behind his coat, which is made of reflective material, sends film to a projector, which bounces the image off the front of the coat — making Obana appear to be transparent.

WOULD YOU BELIEVE?

Funny Money

In Roanoke Rapids, North Carolina, a man used a $200 bill to pay for his groceries on September 6, 2003. Apparently, the cashier was oblivious to the fact that there's no such denomination in USA currency — as well as to the photo of George W. Bush on one side and signs, sporting such slogans as "USA deserves a tax cut," on the White House lawn on the other side.

Hat Trick! When 16-year-old Elsie Wright took photographs of her friend, 11-year-old Frances Griffiths, posing with fairies in Cottingley, England, in 1917, many people regarded the photos as proof that fairies existed. It wasn't until the early 1980s that Wright and Griffiths finally admitted that the fairies were actually cut-out drawings fastened to the ground with hatpins!

Phony Fish Tale

In 1845, a fossil hunter named Albert Koch heard that giant fossilized bones belonging to a sea serpent had been found in Alabama. Koch cobbled together a 114-foot-long skeleton of the creature and took it on tour. Curiosity seekers flocked to see it — at least until scientists pointed out two problems. First, the bones did not belong to a sea serpent but to an ancestor of the whale. Second, Koch had added the vertebrae from five different fossils to make his specimen more impressive. It wasn't the first time, either. In 1844, Koch had sold a skeleton of the "Missourium" — actually an incorrectly assembled mastodon with extra bones — to the British Museum in London!

What a Deal!

When a seller identifying himself as the Emperor of West Virginia listed the "entire state" on eBay, he received 56 bids — the highest of which was just short of $100 million — before eBay shut down the fraudulent auction!

Wasp Sting

On April 1, 1949, Phil Stone, a disk jockey on the radio in New Zealand, had a little fun with his listeners when he warned them that a mile-wide swarm of wasps was headed their way. He advised them not to leave home before pulling their socks up over their pant legs and putting honey-smeared traps outside their doors. Hundreds of gullible listeners did just that!

MOMENTARY MASTERPIECES

Bread-Winner! Six chefs at a hotel in Tokyo, Japan, created a 10-foot-tall, 1,100-pound replica of Godzilla using 14,000 pieces of bread.

Nice Spread

To keep her work from melting, butter sculptor Norma "Duffy" Lyon never works in a room that is warmer than 42 degrees. Every year since 1960, Lyon has carved a life-size cow out of 600 pounds of butter for the annual Iowa State Fair. In recent years, she's added life-size butter sculptures of Elvis Presley, John Wayne, Garth Books, and Leonardo Da Vinci's painting *The Last Supper*.

King Corn

In 2003, to celebrate the 70th anniversary of the original *King Kong* movie, students from Camberwell College in London, England, spent 630 hours building a 13-foot tall, 1,720-pound replica of the giant gorilla — out of popcorn!

Candy Man

Peter Rocha's masterpieces are good enough to eat, but most people wouldn't think of doing any such thing! His jelly-bean mosaics can be seen in Ripley's Odditoriums and in the online Jelly Belly Bean Gallery of the Jelly Belly Candy Company. Among the mosaics is a portrait of the late Ronald Reagan, whose passion for jelly beans was legendary.

Meltin' John

The first chocolate figure to be exhibited at Madame Tussaud's London museum is a sculpture of Elton John. This sweet work of art was made from 277.8 pounds of Cadbury chocolate. To prevent the sun going down on the sculpture and turning Elton John into Meltin' John, the chocolate carving, which took over 1,000 hours to create, is being kept under constant surveillance in its frigid air-conditioned tent.

133

NICE SAVES

Waste — Not!

Since 1990, more than 50 artists have participated in the Artist-in-Residence Program sponsored by SF Recycling & Disposal, Inc., in San Francisco, California. About every three months, up to four artists are selected to pick through trash collected from around the city and turn it into works of art. At the end of the residency, the artists get to display their works in a show open to the public. While Sandy Drobny was a resident in 2004, she turned plastic shopping bags, shower curtains, rubber gloves, and more into wearable art.

Bumper Art! Jon Bedford of New Mexico has created life-size sculptures — including an anaconda, a rhinoceros, and a stegosaurus — from the chrome bumpers of old cars!

Blood Work

British artist Marc Quinn produced *Self*, a sculptural self-portrait of his head made from nine pints of his own frozen, congealed blood that he had harvested over a period of five months!

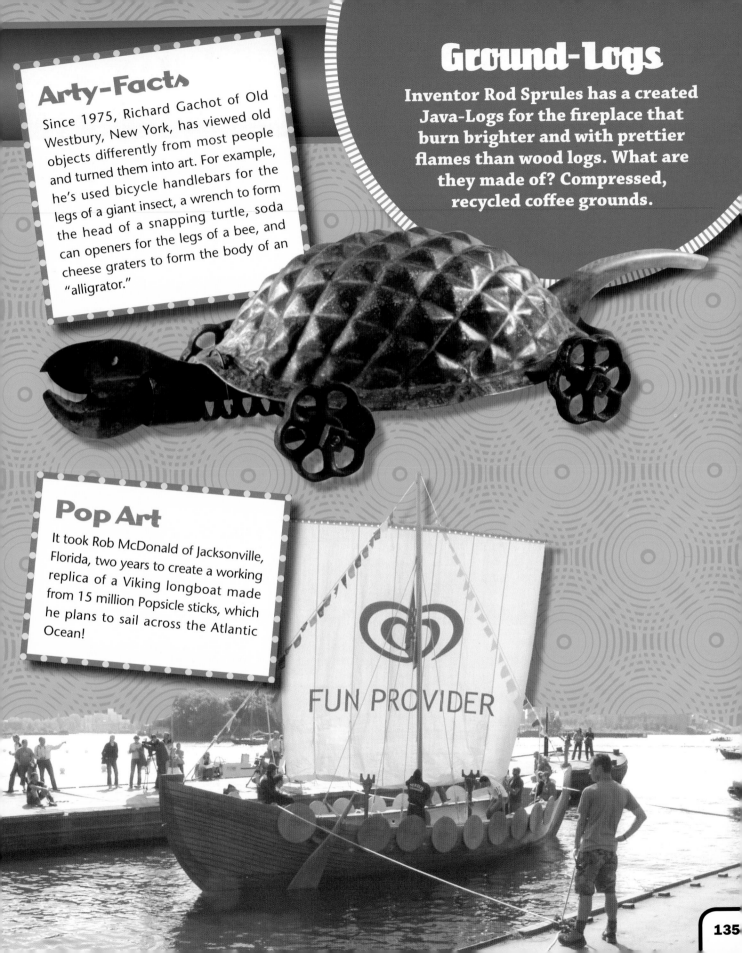

Arty-Facts

Since 1975, Richard Gachot of Old Westbury, New York, has viewed old objects differently from most people and turned them into art. For example, he's used bicycle handlebars for the legs of a giant insect, a wrench to form the head of a snapping turtle, soda can openers for the legs of a bee, and cheese graters to form the body of an "alligator."

Ground-Logs

Inventor Rod Sprules has a created Java-Logs for the fireplace that burn brighter and with prettier flames than wood logs. What are they made of? Compressed, recycled coffee grounds.

Pop Art

It took Rob McDonald of Jacksonville, Florida, two years to create a working replica of a Viking longboat made from 15 million Popsicle sticks, which he plans to sail across the Atlantic Ocean!

FUN PROVIDER

RADICAL ROADSTERS

Peelin' Out!

Terry Axelson of Sunnyville, California, wanted to drive something with a little more style and a lot more *a-peel* than he could buy at a conventional dealership, so he decided to build his own vehicle. Made out of fiberglass and steel, his Banana Bike can reach a speed of 30 miles per hour.

All Buttoned Up

What do you put inside a button-covered hearse? A button-covered coffin, of course! It seems that Dalton "The Button King" Stevens of Bishopville, North Carolina, will cover just about anything with buttons. It all started with a terrible case of insomnia. Rather than lie there doing nothing, Stevens got busy. The result of his nocturnal efforts are a button-covered suit, toilet seat, guitar, American flag, and his crowning achievement — the hearse, which is covered with 600,000 buttons!

RIPLEY FILE:
7.02.1960

Clean Getaway! Jaap Zwart of Amsterdam, The Netherlands, built an automobile out of a bathtub!

Hood-Winked

Sculptor Jud Turner of Eugene, Oregon, likes keeping his artwork right out in front — of cars, that is. Among his many custom hood ornaments are dinosaurs, scorpions, and skulls.

Spinning His Wheel

Kerry McLean of Walled Lake, Michigan, had always dreamed of building a speedy vehicle that was unlike anything that had ever been built before. So when he came up with a V8 gas-powered aluminum monocycle driven from inside the wheel itself, he knew he had achieved his goal. Despite the monocycle's being as big a challenge to ride as it was to build, McLean has ridden it fast enough to set the land speed world record for a single-wheeled vehicle: 53 miles per hour!

Turtle Power

James Riseborough of Boston, Massachusetts, gets a lot of attention when he drives Cecil the Turtle down the street — and that's just the point. His company, aptly named Turtle Transit, transforms ordinary cars into eye-popping advertisements on wheels. Actually, the turtle car is just one of a fleet of head-turners that also includes Elvis the Rhinoceros and a giant pink pig towing two little pigs. It would be hard to find a better way to draw attention to a product.

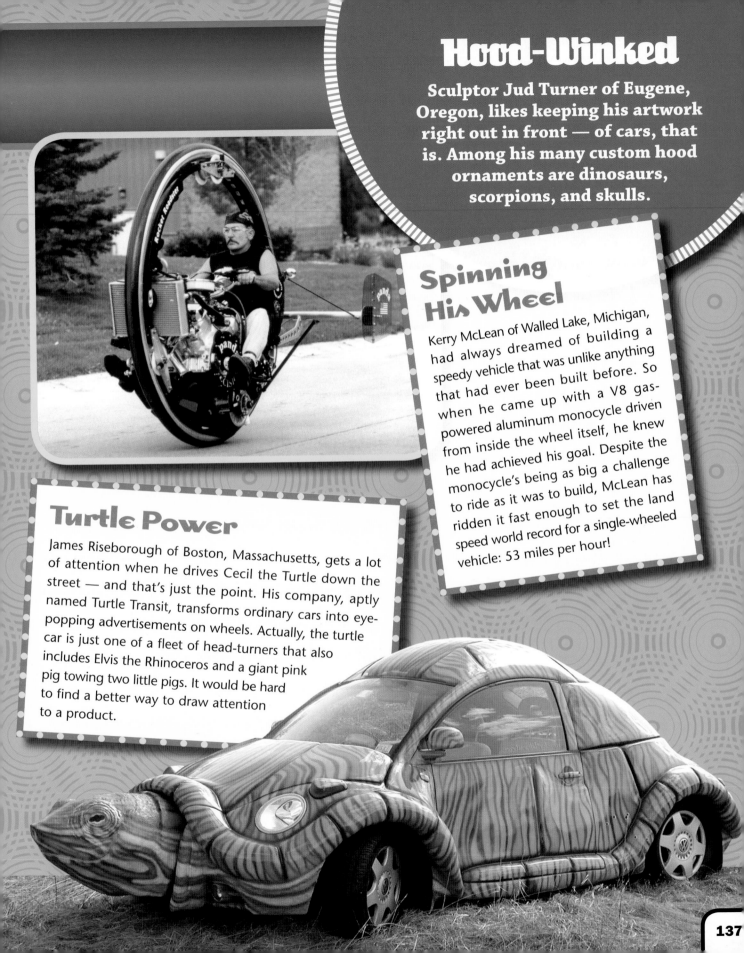

EXTRA! EXTRA!

Salon Teatment

Over a period of four months, Yvonne Millner of Hopkins, South Carolina, used 147 bottles of nail polish to paint her car — which she's named Smiley.

Crack!

Bob Hoke of Scottsdale, Arizona, uses high-speed drills to carve delicate filigree patterns on ostrich eggs, each of which can take up to 400 hours to complete.

Food Drawer

When his pantry needed replenishing, artist Michelangelo (1478–1564) sketched still lifes of wine, fruit, bread, and spaghetti (depending on what he needed) as a shopping list for his illiterate cook.

Designing Women

Your Concept Car (YCC) is a car designed at Volvo by women for women. Once YCC comes on the market, the buyer's body will be scanned at the dealership and the information digitally stored. So when she jumps in the car and inserts her key, the driver's seat, steering wheel, pedals, and seat belt will be automatically adjusted! The car also comes with detachable seat pads that can be removed for washing or changed to a color and style that suits one's mood — and there are compartments for handbags, laptops, cell phones, and more.

Simon Says

Someone wearing what looks like headphones is waking toward you. Then the person suddenly veers to the left before jerking back to the right and almost falls. What's going on? The person's movements are being directed by remote control! The headgear delivers weak jolts of electricity to the area behind the ears, making the person feel off-balance. He or she then tries to compensate by shifting toward the remote control device held by someone else. The technique is called galvanic vestibular stimulation, or GVS. Possible applications include making computer gaming more realistic and helping people with an impaired sense of balance.

Tail-less Tale

A fountain in Bodenwerder, Germany, features a statue of Baron Karl von Münchausen (1720–1797) riding half a horse — a memorial to his tall tale that during the wars between Russia and Turkey, he rode half a horse to victory.

X-treme Shopping

Andy Tyler of Beccles, England, created a jet-propelled shopping cart that is capable of going faster than 50 miles per hour — and it only cost him $90 to make.

Moldy Oldies

In 1928, biochemist Alexander Fleming of Scotland created living paintings using penicillin and bacillus molds on blotting paper!

Shop Talk

GPS (Global Positioning System) may soon be used on shopping carts to suggest recipes and alert customers to special offers, as well as provide them with the quickest route through the store!

INDEX

PHOTO CREDITS: Ripley Entertainment Inc. and the editors of this book wish to thank the following photographers, agents, and other individuals for permission to use and reprint the following photographs in this book. Any photographs included in this book that are not acknowledged below are property of the Ripley Archives. Great effort has been made to obtain permission from the owners of all materials included in this book. Any errors that may have been made are unintentional and will gladly be corrected in future printings if notice is sent to Ripley Entertainment, Inc., 7576 Kingspointe Parkway, Suite 188, Orlando, Florida 32819

COVER: Mummy—Rosanne Pennella; Elaine Davidson—AP Wide World Photos; Sam the Dog—Courtesy Mark Tautrim/www.samugliestdog.com; X ray—Picture Quest; Augie the Dog—Lauren Miller; Monocycle—Courtesy Kerry McLean and Lee Flamard; Gary "Stretch" Turner—Getty Images; Aye Aye—Bristol Zoo

TITLE PAGE: Rajendra Kumar Tiwari—AFP/Getty Images

TOC: Hairstyle—David Yellen; Cecil the Turtle—Courtesy Turtle Transit; Alien—Photonica/Getty Images

PAGE 5: Augie the Dog—Lauren Miller; Zack Phillips—Jack Gescheidt; X ray—Picture Quest

PAGE 6: Mummy—Rosanne Pennella

PAGE 7: Napier-Campbell Bluebird—Motion Picture Library

CHAPTER 1: 9, 15: Kevin Thackwell—Scott Barbour/Getty Images; **10:** Alain Robert—AP/Wide World Photos; Boar—Fotosearch; **11:** Toad Wedding—Reuters; **12:** Balloon Fiesta—Raymond Watt; Elephant Roundup Festival—AP/Wide World Photos; **13:** Ivrea Orange Festival—Courtesy Foto Marino/www.studiocomet.it; Küssnacht Festival—Sonderegger/Viesti Associates; **14:** Staffan Mossenmark Orchestra—AP/Wide World Photos; World Naked Bike Ride—John D. McHugh/AFP/Getty Images; **15:** Cell Phone—Ablestock; **16:** La Sagrada Familia—Neil Setchfield/Art Archive; La Specola—Saulo Bambi/Museo di Storia Naturale sez. Zoologica "La Specola" Firenze; **17:** Germaul—Courtesy Schloss Hellbrunn, Austria; York Maze—Courtesy York Maze; Campbell's Soup Sculpture—Philip J. Bigg/Bigg World Photography; **18:** Cadillac Ranch—Robyn Beck/AFP/Getty Images; Toucan Phone Booth—Paulo Whitaker/Newscom; San Francisco in Jell-O—Elizabeth Hickok; **19:** Replica, Basilica of Saint Peter, Rome—Reuters; **21:** Policeman's Hat—Ablestock

CHAPTER 2: 23, 28: Anglerfish—E. Widder/ORCA; **24:** *Deep Impact* Spacecraft—NASA Kennedy Space Center (NASA/KSC); Asteroid Impact—Don Davis, Artist/NASA; **25:** Xena—NASA Jet Propulsion Laboratory (NASA-JPL); Alien—Photonica/Getty Images; **26:** Volcano—Ablestock; *Armillaria ostoyae* Fungus—G.W. Hudler, Plant Pathology, Cornell University; **27:** Turquoise—Biophoto Associates/Photo Researchers; Amethyst—Mark A. Schneider/Photo Researchers; Garnet—Mark A. Schneider/Photo Researchers; Opal—Charles D. Winters/Photo Researchers; Aquamarine—M. Claye/Jacana/Photo Researchers; **28:** Tubeworms—C. Van Dorn/OAR/National Undersea Research Program, College of William and Mary/NOAA; **29:** Black Smokers—P. Rona/OAR/National Undersea Research Program/NOAA; Giant Larvacean—Image Quest 3-D; **30:** Galaxy—NASA; **31:** Moon—Ablestock

CHAPTER 3: 33, 37: Dubble Bubble Contest—Newscom; **34:** Danny Way—Jason Lee/RKR/KI China/Reuters; **35:** Felix Baumgartner—Bernard Spoettel/AFP/Getty Images; Jürgen Köhler—Courtesy Alexander Bont; **36:** Ticket Masters—Courtesy Summit, New Jersey, Detective Bureau, Police Department; **37:** Katie Brownell—Icon SMI/Newscom; **38:** Forensics Class—Bobby Coker/Orlando Sentinel; Jeff Payne—Brian Kersey/AP/Wide World Photos; **39:** Civil Rights Documentary—Nam Huh/AP Wide World Photos; **40:** Naked Rambler—Andrew Milligan/EPA Photos/Newscom; Rajendra Kumar Tiwari—AFP/Getty

Images; **41:** Nur Malena Hassan—Jimin Lai/AFP/Getty Images; Ellen MacArthur—Malcolm Clark/Zuma Press/Newscom; **42:** Juggler—Ablestock; **43:** Coffee Beans—Ablestock

CHAPTER 4: 45: St. Petersburg Bridge Hairstyle—Alexander Demianchuk/Reuters; **46:** Isobel Varley—Courtesy Bryan Nye; **47:** Garry "Stretch" Turner—Scott Barbour/Getty Images; Zack Phillips—Jack Gescheidt; **48:** Helicopter Hairstyle—David Yellen; **49:** Hairstyle—David Yellen; Moscow's Red Square Hairstyle—Alexander Demianchuk/Reuters; **50:** Dudu Miah—Rafiqur Rahman/Reuters; **51:** Insect Inter—Porchai Kitti Wong Sakul/AFP/Getty Images; Man with Witchetty Grub—Patrick Horton/Painet, Inc.; **52:** Dirtiest Kid Contest—John T. Baar/AFP/Getty Images; **53:** Finger-Pullers—Dieter Endlicher/AP Wide World Photos; Bridezilla—Diane Bondanareff/AP Wide World Photos; **54:** Louisville Slugger Museum—© Hillerich & Bradsby Co.; Western Boot Factory—Andrew Hempstead; **55:** World's Largest Tomahawk—David Baker/Courtesy Saskatchewan Centennial; World's Longest Sofa—Anwar Mirza/Reuters; **56:** Koala, Chicken—Ablestock

CHAPTER 5: 59, 60: Dog Rescue, Hurricane Katrina—Mario Tama/Getty Images; **60:** Bob Weston—Howard Schnapp; **61:** Helicopter Rescue—SABC/APTN/AP Wide World Photos; Sofia Pedro and Daughter—Karel Prinsloo/AP Wide World Photos; **62:** Michael Utley—Courtesy Michael Utley; Silhouette and Lightning—Ablestock; Cliff Meidl—Allsport/Mark Dadswell/Getty Images; **63:** Electrocuted Bear—Greg Sorber/*Albuquerque Journal*; **64:** Richard Van Pham's Sailboat—Courtesy U.S. Navy; Muhammet Kalem—Ihlas News Agency/Reuters; **65:** Brennan Hawkins—Kent Horner/AP Wide World Photos; **66:** Water—Ablestock; Copperhead Snake—U.S. Fish and Wildlife Service; **67:** Squirrel—Ablestock

CHAPTER 6: 69: Tarsier—G. Ronald Austing/Photo Researchers; **70:** Sam the Dog—Courtesy Mark Tautrim; Tarsier—Tom McHugh/Photo Researchers; **71:** Star-Nosed Mole—Gary Meszaros; Aye-Aye—Rob Cousins/Getty Images; **72:** Scorpion—John Visser; Firefly—Darwin Dale/Photo Researchers; **73:** Blister Beetle—Nature's Images/Photo Researchers; Spittlebug—James A. Robinson/Photo Researchers; **74:** Baboons—David Hosking/Photo Researchers; **74:** Gorillas—Brand X Pictures/Newscom; **75:** Dolphin, Elephant—Ablestock; **76:** Hippopotamus—Ablestock; Marine Cone Snail—Norbert Wu/Minden Pictures; **77:** Poison Dart Frog—Michael Lustbader/Photo Researchers; Burmese Python and Alligator—Everglades National Park/AP Wide World Photos; **78:** Botok and Mother—THINKFilm, Inc.; Muschi and Mäuschen—Alexander Ruesche/Landov; **79:** Saimai and Piglets—Barbara Walton/EPA/Landov; Owen and Mzee—Peter Greste/PRN News Photo/Scholastic/Newscom; **80:** Cats—L. C. Casterline

CHAPTER 7: 83, 87: Capuchin Mummies—William Albert Allard/National Geographic/Getty Images; **84:** King Tut Statue—Egyptian Supreme Council of Antiquities/AP Wide World Photos; Forensic Reconstruction of King Tut—National Geographic; **85:** Inuit Mummy—National Museum, Greenland; Natalia Polosmak and Ice Maiden Mummy—National Geographic; **86:** Man Cleaning Skulls—Surkee Supklang/Reuters; Skull—Ablestock; **88:** George Washington's Deathbed—North Wind Picture Archives; Abraham Lincoln's Funeral Train—Art Archive; John Adams—Chateau de Blerancourt/Dagli

Orti/Art Archive; James Garfield Assassination—Culver Pictures/Art Archive; **89:** William Henry Harrison Inauguration—Library of Congress; Parrot—Ablestock; Zachary Taylor—Chateau de Blerancourt/Dagli Orti/Art Archive; JFK Funeral—Art Archive; **90:** Swollen Toad—Florian Quand/AP Wide World Photos; Locusts in Yucatan—Jose Acosta/AP Wide World Photos; **91:** Toothbrush, Raw Meat, Telephone, Vacuum Cleaner—Ablestock; Toothpaste Surface, Sponge Bacteria—Eye o Science/Photo Researchers; Rhinovirus—JY-SGRO/Phot Researchers; Dust Mites—CNRI/Photo Researchers; **92:** Fireworks—Ablestock; **93:** Bugle—Ablestock; Pet Tombstone—L. C. Casterline

CHAPTER 8: 96: Seeing with Sound—Bryan Christie Design; **97:** Liquid Trust—Courtesy Verolabs.com; P. Read Montague—© 2005 Agapito Sanchez, Baylor College of Medicine; **98:** Newborns—Joe Klamar/Getty Images; Firefly—Dr. Paul A. Zahl; **99:** Mark Roth—© 2005 Fred Hutchinson Cancer Research Center; Mouse—Juergen Koch/Minden Pictures; **100–101:** Boy on Bicycle—Fotosearch; **100:** Teeth, Brain—Ablestock; **101:** Heart—Fotosearch; Hand Bones—Ablestock; **102:** Pocket Monsters (Pokémon)—Kyodo News Photo; John Evans—Sony Pictures Television; **103:** Twins—WorldWideFeatures.com; **106:** Clown, Petri Dish—Ablestock; **107:** Surgical Instrument—Ablestock

CHAPTER 9: 109, 115: African Grey Parrot—Stephen Dalton/Photo Researchers, Inc.; **110:** Lily Dale—Larry Anderson; Black Abbot—Fortean Picture Library; **111:** Psychic Katie—Fortean Picture Library; **112:** Mary Russell Mitford—Granger; Dice, Money—Ablestock; **113:** Donna Goeppert—Michael Kobel/*The Morning Call*/AP Wide World Photos; Lottery Tumbler, Money—Ablestock; **114:** David Mandell—Guy Levy; **115:** Albert Trevino—Toby Canham/Splash News/Newscom

CHAPTER 10: 121, 133: Chocolate Elton John—Carl de Zousa/Getty Images; **122:** Electronic Eyewear—Michael Springer/Getty Images; Merry-go-round Water Pump—Schlak van Zuydam/AP Wide World Photos; **123:** Dolphin Watercraft—Mandy Marie/Innespace Productions; **124:** Pivo Concept Car—Getty Images News; Batmobile—AP Wide World Photos; **125:** Les Wong—Henry Lai/Ovahere.com; Les Wong's Mazda RX-7—Courtesy Les Wong; **126:** Napier-Campbell Bluebird, Blue Flame—Motoring Picture Library; Thrust SSC II—Jeremy Davey/SSC Programme Ltd./Getty Images; **127:** Campbell Railton Rolls-Royce Bluebird, Craig Breedlove and Spirit of America, Spirit of America Sonic 1—Motoring Picture Library; **128:** Intellifit—Getty Images; **129:** Build Your Own Bag—Courtesy The MIT Media Lab; Invisible Coat—Shizuo Tachi/AP Wide World Photos; **130:** Koch Sea Serpent—Strangescience.net and Richard Ellis, *Monsters of the Sea*, NY: Alfred A. Knopf, 1954; **131:** Wasp—Kenneth H. Thomas/Photo Researchers; **132:** Lauren Duffy's *The Last Supper*—Layne Kennedy/Time & Life Pictures/Getty Images; **133:** Ronald Reagan Jelly Bean Portrait—Courtesy Jelly Belly Candy Company; **134:** *Corazon Tejido* by Sandy Drobny—Courtesy Michael Kerbow/S.F. Recycling & Disposal, Inc.; Self by Marc Quinn—Lynsey Addario/AP Wide World Photos; **135:** *Snapping Turtle* by Richard Gachot—Courtesy Richard Gachot; **136:** Banana Bike—Terry Axelton/Art Car Agency; "The Button King"—Dalton Stevens/Art Car Agency; **137:** Monocycle—Courtesy Kerry McLean and Lee Flamard; Cecil the Turtle—Courtesy Turtle Transit; **138:** Drill, Food, Wine Bottle—Ablestock

PHOTO RESEARCH: Carousel Research, Inc.